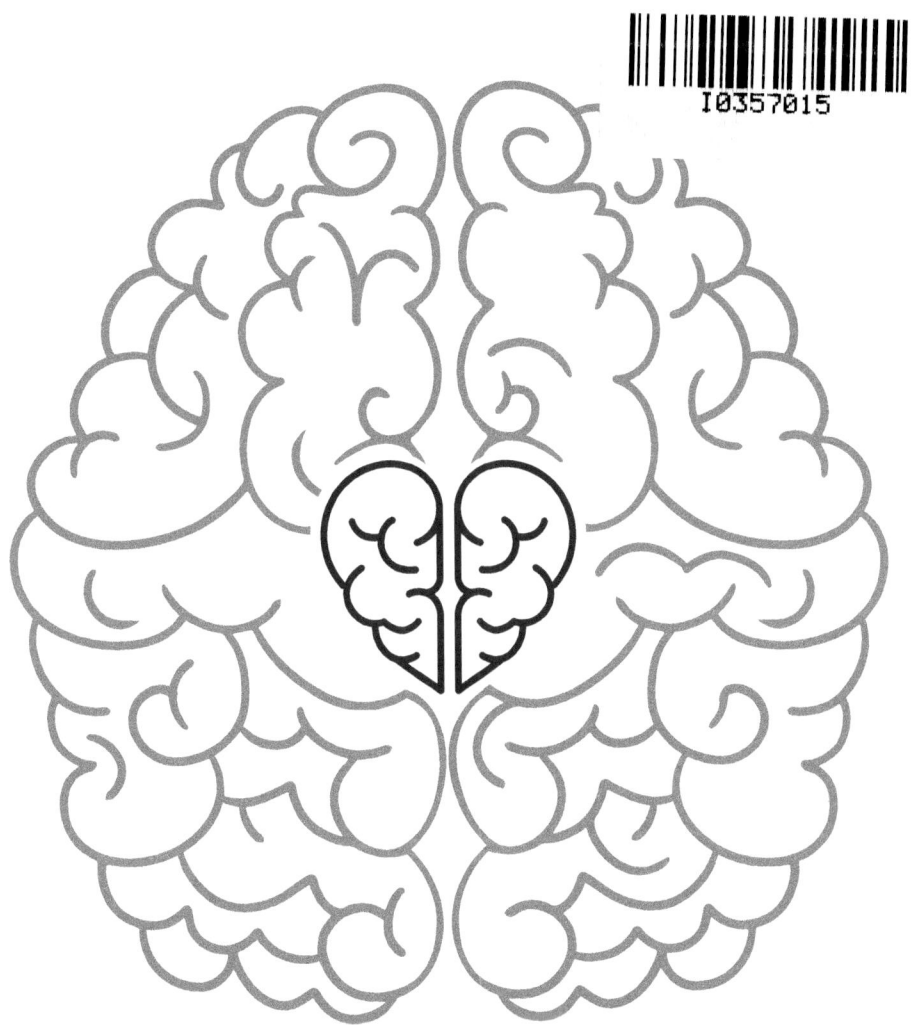

THINK LIKE JESUS
And see the future first

Dr Kobus Neethling | Prof Hennie Stander | Dr Raché Rutherford

© 2023 MyLife® Group Holdings
Trent Bridge Office Park,
Block B, 1st Floor,
Cnr Leonie Str & Von Willich Ave,
Doringkloof,
Centurion,
0157

Tel: 012 942 5111
E-mail: books@mylife.co.za
First edition, first print 2000

Book layout and cover design: Christina Harman
Printed and bound by IngramSpark

ISBN: 978-0-7961-0723-7 (print)
        978-0-7961-0724-4 (e-book)

© All rights reserved. No part of this book may be reproduced in any form without permission in writing from the publisher.

THINK LIKE JESUS
And see the future first

Dr Kobus Neethling | Prof Hennie Stander | Dr Raché Rutherford

CONTENTS

PREFACE
In the Word and after the Word i

ONE
To understand before we understand 1

TWO
Jesus' thinking processes in action 9

THREE
The metaphor: Your joyful fountains are within 33

FOUR
Paradox: The opposite of the truth can be the truth 47

FIVE
Intuition – To know before you know 57

SIX
Image streaming – To see the world in a grain of sand and heaven in the yellow of the sunflower 69

SEVEN
System thinking – When the butterfly flaps its wings in Miami, it hails in Beijing 81

EIGHT
"Out of the box" thinking – Every exit is an entrance to something else 93

NINE
Whole brain thinking – To look with a fresh pair of eyes 107

TEN
Jesus' model for the 21st century 119

PREFACE

In the Word and after the Word

As the tempo of development escalates at an alarming rate and all projections indicate that the tempo will remain breathtakingly fast, the question automatically arises: What should the 21st-century human being be like so that he/she could manage the speed waves with creative ease and dignity? Every new generation evaluates, adapts, and renews the guidelines for staying ahead. Undoubtedly, new directives and guidelines are being sought urgently today, and will be sought tomorrow and in the decades to come.

The authors identified some of the most exceptional achievers through the ages and attempted to find out how they thought before they acted. The premise for this approach is that if we can gain insight into their thinking processes, it will shed additional and new light on creative problem-solving and help provide innovative solutions for creating 21st-century opportunities.

Therefore, if one looks for new possibilities in one's relationships, personal and professional circumstances, business, parenting, education, sport, and ministry, and one asks the question: How would Einstein, Da Vinci or Edison (or any other extraordinary thinker) have approached the challenge, insights into thinking processes become essential — it becomes a critical issue.

Jesus as an extraordinary person was confronted with every possible kind of challenge:
Relationships with:

- God
- fellow human beings
- the state
- circumstances
- himself

Relationships involving:
- perceptions of God
- leadership
- management
- parenting
- education (doctrine)
- traditions (customs)
- money
- business
- status (position in society)
- team building
- value system
- outsiders ('scum' of the earth)
- death

In each of the above-mentioned contexts, Jesus was challenged to act creatively, and meaningfully. Often His thinking was challenged to the extreme. Thus, it becomes absolutely critical to determine Jesus' thinking preferences so that we can understand His actions more clearly. We are convinced that, if we could determine how someone thinks and which thinking processes are created, we would be able to emulate those processes and teach them to others.

Furthermore, we are of the opinion that when you imitate positive behaviour, it can lead to an improvement in your own behaviour. For example, as an inexperienced teacher at a school, I can improve and hone my own teaching skills creatively by continually observing and emulating an experienced, innovative teacher. In-depth insight, however, occurs only when I gain an understanding of the creative thinking processes of that teacher and how he/she keeps changing and renewing his/her thinking to handle different situations. I have unique characteristics, but I can only become as successful as him/her when I can 'enter' his/her brain and understand the thinking before the acting.

This is true of the world-changing acts of Jesus – and the Bible explicitly indicates that man's renewal – 'to become a different person' – happens in his/her thinking and nowhere else. The writers are convinced that one can make certain deductions from the Bible about Jesus' way of thinking and that these insights (no matter how limited because of our human limitations), hold boundless possibilities for every human being. The authors are deeply conscious of the fact that the primary aim of the Bible is not to serve as a textbook on creativity. First and foremost, its role is to inform man about how to mend his/her broken relationship with God. The authors are also conscious of the fact that one should be very cautious when making these deductions because Jesus himself never wrote anything. The sources we use are derived from various Evangelists who each had his own objective in writing his Gospel. Nevertheless, based on their writings, it is possible to form a very clear idea of Jesus' thinking. The practical exercises at the end of the book are not necessarily the theological applications of the particular Scriptures discussed in the different chapters. They are simply modern applications and techniques of the kind of thinking Jesus applied.

Dr. Kobus Neethling, dr. Raché Rutherford and Prof. Hennie Stander teamed up to give this book, from a theological as well as a creativity perspective, a scientific grounding. Dr. Kobus Neethling, internationally recognised as a creative expert, and dr. Raché Rutherford have written more than 60 books. Prof. Hennie Stander was a lecturer in the Department of Ancient Languages (University of Pretoria) and is the author and co-author of more than 50 books and chapters in books, and more than 400 popular and academic articles. These three writers aimed at writing a book which, through its content and approach, could serve as an illuminating guide to every child and adult on their journey through life. Although the approaches and methods used by the authors are based completely on the Bible, the writers trust that this book will not only be a book for the church but that it will be a very special thinking and doing guide for every person in search of meaning and creative wisdom. In all modesty we believe that the book, because of its innovative, creative search for manifestations of the truth, will serve as an introductory work for approaching any new challenge life brings.

In the chapters that follow we first explain the models we used to arrive at the essence of Jesus' thinking. Subsequently, we focus on the seven thinking techniques Jesus gave preference to and we attempt to deduce what His thinking profile looked like. In the final chapter we discuss the implications of Jesus' thinking for every individual and group facing life's challenges:

- parents
- teachers
- ministers of religion
- sports people
- entrepreneurs

Jesus constantly used His whole brain, although He often demonstrated special thinking preferences. We also try to determine the implications of these preferences for the people of our times.

The two masterpieces of Laurie Beth Jones: Jesus CEO: Using Ancient Wisdom for Visionary Leadership (1995), and Jesus in Blue Jeans (1997) brought particular insights into the style and conduct of Jesus. Charles C. Manz's Leadership Wisdom of Jesus (1997) was a call to follow His passionate and wise leadership style. Paul Avis's The Resurrection of Jesus Christ (1993) and God and the Creative Imagination (1999), are revealing publications focusing on the unique qualities of God and Jesus. They also shed meaningful and innovative light on the life and works of Jesus.

We believe that in this book we are drawing a connecting line between Jesus' life and conduct and His thinking that preceded His actions. Think like Jesus is, in our opinion, as strong a directive to be followed as Do like Jesus and Follow Jesus' example have always been.

God as the supreme Creator wants us to be creative – He gave us Jesus as an example and He gave us a brain with which to create. If we want to be like Jesus, we will have to start thinking like Jesus.

> *" In the beginning,*
> *God created the heavens and the earth. "*
>
> **– Genesis 1:1**

ONE

TO UNDERSTAND BEFORE WE UNDERSTAND

Studies of exceptional achievers like Da Vinci, Michelangelo, Einstein and others indicate that if one could understand their thinking processes, it would be possible to teach these processes, to emulate them and eventually gain a unique insight into their creations and achievements. In this chapter we try to discover Jesus' thinking processes and try to understand the essence of His thinking.

Jesus' Actions and Being and the miracles He performed, His conduct, teaching, communication, etc., have been the central focus of historians, scripturalists, text analysts and students of theology for the past 2000 years. Psychological and sociological studies have provided further insights regarding the Doing and Being of Jesus. Through the ages these research methods have brought remarkable revelations and are still contributing to fascinating insights.

Perhaps it is necessary to add a new dimension – a different angle, another filter that will not dispel the mystery, but shed more light on how to cope in a century that will not suffer ordinary, mundane thinking. What you think and how you think eventually determine what you become. Your thinking from birth up till now has determined who and what you are today. Your thinking today and tomorrow determines what you will become in future.

What comes out of your mouth has been processed in your brain. We are convinced that unique insights can be gained into the miracles of Jesus, His teachings, His communication, His solving of problems if we can determine more clearly how Jesus thought.

Because we regard thinking as the central point of departure to understand behaviour, we are of the opinion that Jesus must serve as the perfect guide, as the ultimate thinking example. The Bible focuses in special ways on thinking as the central source of renewal.

In Romans 12:2 Paul says: *"Do not conform outwardly to the standards of this world, but let God transform you inwardly by a complete change of your mind."*

This text puts it negatively first, then positively. Paul asks that we shall not continue doing what the people do who live without Jesus. How does one break away from the norm of everyday life? How does one succeed in following a completely new direction? Paul puts it positively: By starting to think differently about things. One must allow God to help one start thinking differently. When one thinks in a different way, one starts acting in a different way.

In 1 Corinthians 14:20 Paul says: *"Do not be like children in your thinking, brothers; be children so far as evil is concerned, but be mature in your thinking."*

When we grow in our thinking, we start acting differently. Our thinking determines our future actions.

In 1 Peter 1:13 we read: *"Therefore gird up the loins of your mind, be sober, and rest your hope fully upon the grace that is to be brought to you at the revelation of Jesus Christ."*

In ancient times people wore long robes. When they got up to walk or to work, they tied the robe with a belt round their waists. The expression 'to gird up the loins' became idiomatic for 'getting ready'. What Peter means is that one has to 'gird' one's mind – i.e. 'get it geared'. Thus he appeals to his readers to fix their thinking on something else – on a future dream! When Christ comes again we shall enjoy the privilege to be in heaven with Him forever. If one renews one's thinking and focuses on this wonderful dream of the future, one's life on earth will take a different turn.

In order to gain further insight into Jesus' wisdom, His leadership, and His influence as the eternity-teacher, it is important to explore the essence of His thinking. Thinking and/or feeling precede action or behaviour. Therefore behaviour is the result of a thinking and feeling process. Christ has been observed, analysed and studied according to the ways in which He behaved towards the people and the world of His time. But so much deeper insight is gained when one probes His thinking before His doing.

Jesus' way of thinking

The following seven examples are indicative of how Jesus acted in different situations. Subsequently we try to determine His thinking processes before His actions in an attempt to get a glimpse of the unseeable. Like us, Jesus also had thinking preferences for each situation, person or problem He was confronted with. These thinking preferences gave rise to His behaviour as recorded in the four Gospels. Our research has indicated that Jesus had specific thinking preferences and preferred specific thinking techniques.

The seven examples we have selected are clear indications of His thinking preferences:

1. Jesus drives the traders from the temple (John 2:14-17)
2. He heals the man with the deformed hand (Mark 3:1-5)
3. Jesus and the little children (Mark 10:13-16)
4. He heals a paralysed man (Luke 5:17-26)
5. The question about paying taxes (Luke 20:21-26)
6. The adulterous woman (John 8:1-11)
7. The Sermon on the Mount (Matt. 4:25; 5:1-12; 7:25-29)

The Brain process:

(The traditional process   >)
(Possible deviations   >)

Explanation of process

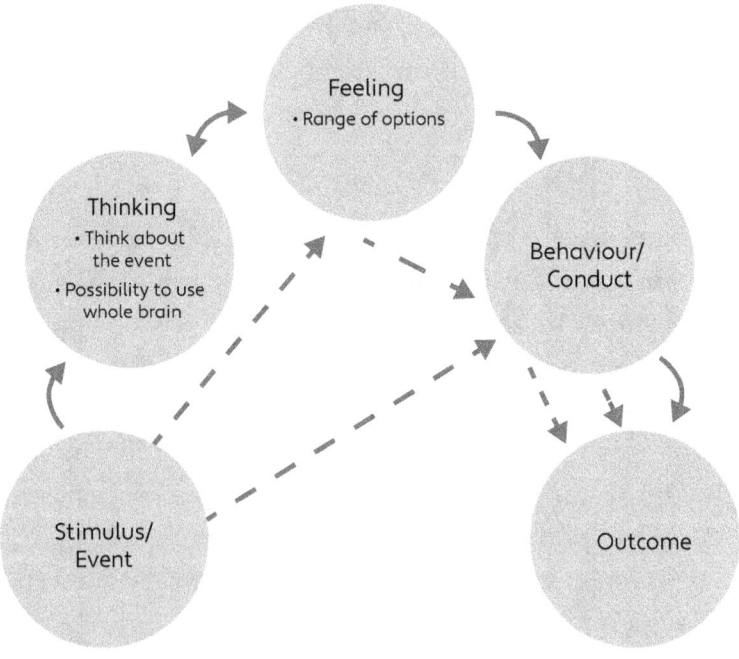

- The brain reacts to a stimulus or event (this stimulus can be a conscious action, or can originate in the sub- or super-consciousness).
- In the traditional process a person's thinking will be activated by a stimulus (or a feeling which is then supported by his/her thinking).
- When thinking then interacts with feelings, it leads to behaviour or action.
- Behaviour is the result of an integration of the thinking and feeling processes.
- Behaviour leads to outcomes that can be observed (by the person himself and/or others who experience or observe the outcome.)

It is possible that the stimulus may trigger instant feelings and then behaviour, without the person's thinking playing any part at all. Here we often talk of emotional hijacking: for example a parent who gets furious (feeling) about a child's behaviour (stimulus) and then slaps the child (behaviour). When we do not allow our thinking to play a part, the outcome is often catastrophic. Or the outcome may often be particularly limited.

You listen to a speech or a sermon (stimulus) and you get emotionally excited (feeling) so that you leave the room or the church determined to go and change the world (behaviour), but soon the impact diminishes and after a few days you are back to where you were (outcome).

When thinking is left out of the brain process, impact and meaning often dissipate.

Practical application

Let us approach this traditional process in a practical way:

A salesperson (stimulus) tries to sell you a computer. Your thinking analyses what he/she says about the advantages of the computer and you start feeling quite positive about it. You decide you want the computer and immediately buy this new product on the market (behaviour). You start using the computer and feel very satisfied with it (outcome).

One can apply this process to almost any facet of one's life: to one's parenting (the parent as stimulus and the children's thinking as point of departure), to the education process, to business, politics, and so forth e.g. your child feels ill (stimulus). Your thinking determines through analysis that he/she might have the flu. You feel slightly worried and take him/her to the doctor (behaviour) who diagnoses the flu, prescribes medicine and he/she starts to improve (outcome).

But it is important to understand that even the traditional thinking process (stimulus – thinking – feeling – behaviour – outcome) may give rise to negative behaviour and outcomes. This is possible because our thinking about situations and circumstances may be negative and problem-focused, which causes a chain reaction of negative feelings and behaviour, and therefore negative outcomes. For example:

You see people whispering (stimulus), you think they are talking about you and you feel upset about it. You become negative (behaviour) and you lose confidence (outcome).

When we tried to apply this model to Jesus, we found that He was first and foremost a solution finder – and not a problem solver. The world around Him, the crowds, the tax collectors, His disciples, the children, the sick and His Father in heaven were the stimuli that brought action to His thinking. Because He focused on a solution in each situation, because His thinking was in a *"searching for positive answers"* mode, we can still today marvel about the outcomes of His behaviour. We believe that such a perspective brings other kinds of insights into the extraordinary ways in which Jesus handled His world. What is also important to us, are the insights we could gain from this study of His thinking and how it equips us to deal with the 21st century in new and creative ways. Jesus managed His circumstances with extraordinary creativity – and created guidelines that are now more relevant than ever before.

> *"Remember to welcome strangers in your homes. There were some who did it and welcomed angels without knowing it."*
>
> **– Hebrews 12:2**

Dr Kobus Neethling | Prof Hennie Stander | Dr Raché Rutherford

TWO

JESUS' THINKING PROCESSES IN ACTION

In this chapter:

- we discuss seven examples of Jesus' thinking in very different circumstances
- we elaborate on the importance of gaining insights into the essence of Jesus' thinking
- we focus on the importance of Jesus' thinking for every person living in the 21st century

Let us analyse seven examples of Jesus' thinking in seven different sets of circumstances. What is remarkable about these kinds of analyses is that it becomes very clear that Jesus' thinking focused on solutions while so many around Him merely focused on the problems.

Till the end of the 20th century most processes and models in the business world, education, sport and even the church, aimed at solving problems. We believe that this emphasis on problems that needed to be solved, led to problem thinking, a problem climate in organisations and eventually to a problem mentality. Furthermore, this problem mentality forced communities, societies and even continents into narrow-mindedness.

Jesus never created a problem climate – He was the Creator of possibilities and solutions. The problem was only a starting point, never the end.

Jesus drove the traders from the temple

John 2:14-17

14. In the temple courts he found men selling cattle, sheep, and doves, and others sitting at tables exchanging money.

15. So he made a whip out of cords, and drove all from the temple area, both sheep and cattle; he scattered the coins of the money changers and overturned their tables. Jesus made a whip from some ropes and chased them all out of the temple.

16. To those who sold doves he said, 'Get these out of here! How dare you turn my father's house into a market!'

17. His disciples remembered that it is written: 'Zeal for your house will consume me.' Or as it is put in the NLT, 'Passion for God's house burns within me.'

A short background

In the temple there was a courtyard built for the heathen because non-Jews were not allowed to enter the inner sanctuary. In this courtyard non-Jews could take part in the Jewish religious practices. The scene of the story about Jesus and the traders that He drove out, is set in this courtyard.

The money changers demanded excessive interest on their transactions, and the traders in sacrificial animals 'loaded' their prices unashamedly so that it was almost impossible for the temple-goers to worship God – which was the actual purpose of their visit. Of course with all the stalls, money tables and noise in the courtyard it became impossible for non-Jews to worship the God of the Jews there.

Jesus' brain process (1)
He drives the traders from the temple

Jesus restores the sanctity of the temple:
explanation

Jesus' reaction to the violators of the temple is remarkable and extraordinary. The violators activate His thinking. He does not become upset and He is not emotionally hijacked like most people would be in similar situations. It is His thinking brain that dominates. He sees the big picture of what is happening in the temple and realises there are various kinds of violators. He thinks strategically and connects His big picture thinking with His passion for His Father's house. Only then follows His well-structured and systematic actions:

1. making the whip
2. driving the stock traders out
3. driving the cattle and sheep out
4. scattering the money
5. overturning the tables
6. carrying out the doves (not throwing them out – obviously more sympathetic behaviour towards the frailty of the doves and sensitive to the sellers of the doves)

From right brain thinking processes that observe and consider everything simultaneously, to the practical, structured, left brain thinking and acting. Jesus' whole brain thinking leads to the sanctity of the temple being restored.

Healing of the man with the deformed hand
What it takes to have a wealth mindset

Mark 3:1-5

1. Jesus went into the synagogue again and noticed a man with a deformed hand.

2. Since it was the Sabbath Jesus' enemies watched him closely. Would he heal the man's hand on the Sabbath? If he did, they planned to condemn him.

3. Jesus said to the man, *"Come and stand in front of everyone."*

4. Then he turned to His critics and asked, *"Is it legal to do good deeds on the Sabbath, or is it a day for doing harm? Is this a day to save life or to destroy it?"* But they wouldn't answer him.

5. He looked around at them angrily, because he was deeply disturbed by their hard hearts. Then he said to the man, *"Reach out your hand."* The man reached out his hand and it became normal again! (NLT)

Jesus' brain process (2)
The man with the deformed hand

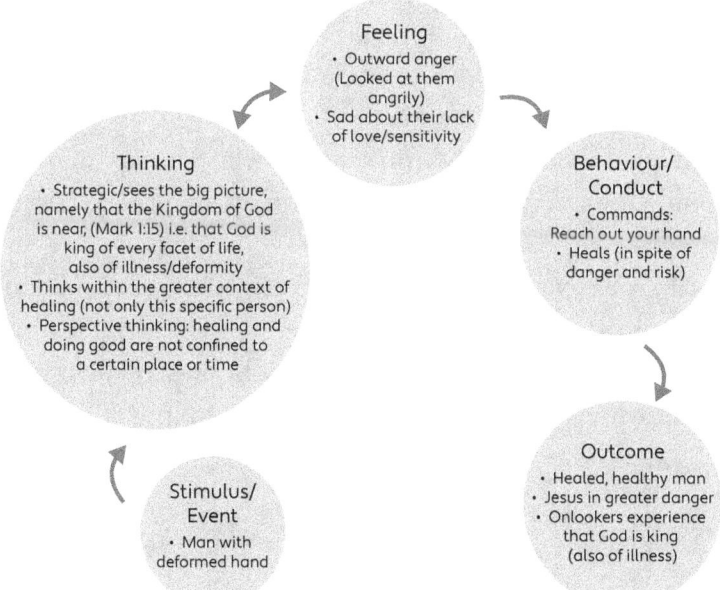

Healing of the man with the deformed hand
explanation

On this particular Sabbath Jesus sees the man with the deformed hand and in a unique way, He sees the big picture within which the story will unfold. Because of the limited, closed thinking of the Pharisees they judge merely by the strict conditions of the law, but Jesus sees the wider context of right and wrong. The big picture Jesus proclaims is that the Kingdom of God is near (Mark 1:15).

"Kingdom of God" means that God is king of every facet of life. Jesus also notices that love for your fellow human beings (in this case the man with the deformed hand) is more important than obeying laws. (In this case the laws regarding the Sabbath).

He tells the man to stand in their midst, so that what will follow will take place openly, in public. His strategic thinking does not only remarkably encompass the different elements of the drama, but also manifests itself masterly in feelings and behaviour:

1. He addresses the issues of good and bad
2. He expresses feelings of sympathetic anger – He is sorry that their hearts are hard and cold
3. Having established the context, He tells the man to extend his hand (Jesus applies the perfect sequencing of the action steps)

Once again it is clear that Jesus has used His strategic right brain that enables Him to see the big picture; then spontaneous feelings and emotions follow. Thereafter comes the left brain structuring and the practical illustration of His precise, focused thinking.

Jesus and the Children

Mark 3:1-5

^{1.} One day some parents brought their children to Jesus so he could touch them and bless them, but the disciples told them not to bother him.

^{2.} But when Jesus saw what was happening, he was very displeased with his disciples. He said to them, *"Let the children come to me. Don't stop them! For the Kingdom of God belongs to such as these."*

^{3.} *"I assure you, anyone who doesn't have their kind of faith will never get into the Kingdom of God."*

^{4.} Then he took the children into His arms and placed His hands on their heads and blessed them. (NLT)

A short background

In ancient times children had no rights. No decent man would ever pay attention in public to children or women. It was simply beneath you to do so. However, Jesus' behaviour was in many ways revolutionary – He never allowed social norms to restrict Him. In those days children were entirely at the mercy of their parents' goodwill. They were completely dependent on their parents. For this reason Jesus uses these children as models for adults. If one wants to enter the Kingdom of God, one has to be like these children who are completely dependent on their parents for their livelihood. Jesus wants the same from us – that we build our entire existence on Him. We must live in complete dependence on Him alone.

Jesus' brain process (3)
Jesus and the children

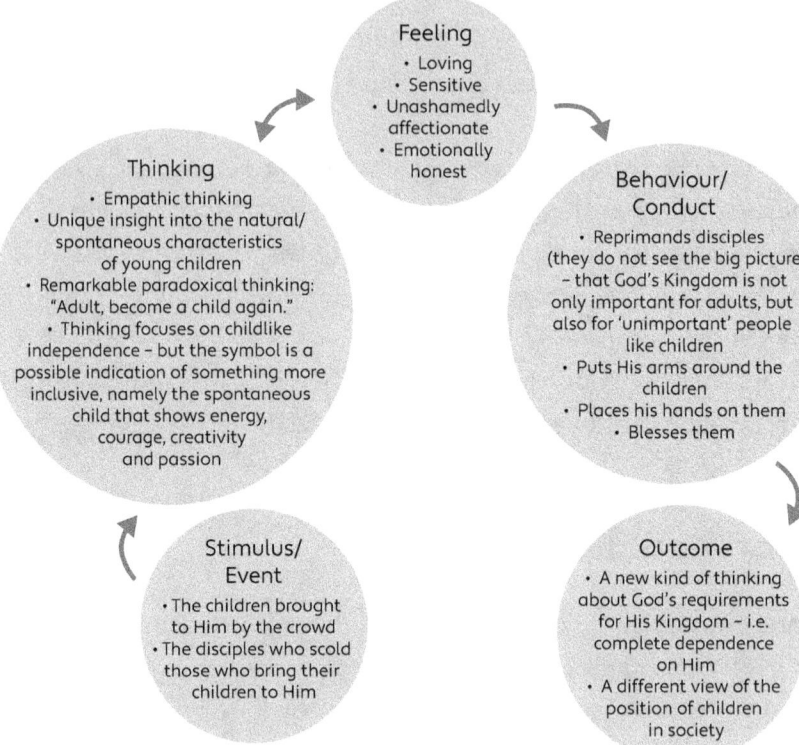

Jesus and the children:
explanation

This classic event that has stayed as fresh and new for thousands of years, illustrates once again Jesus' remarkable powers of thinking in a situation that had the potential for serious conflict.

It is abundantly clear that the disciples do not grasp the essence of the being of a child nor the symbolic value of the children. Jesus defies the social norms of His time and publicly pays attention to these children. His thinking also bears witness of the most sensitive insight into the being and position of the child in the ancient world. A child had no rights and was completely dependent on his/her parents for his/her livelihood. Jesus sees the big picture: God's 'right of admission' is in line with the child's position in society. He demands that one should build one's whole life on God – be dependent on Him alone. He uses paradox-thinking – the apparent contradiction: adult you will have to become like a child. To Jesus this is not a contradiction; to the onlookers it means a paradigm shift to make the apparently impossible possible.

This intuitive big picture thinking of His right brain once again leads to the step-by-step execution of an action plan:
1. He sensitively reprimands His disciples because they lack big picture insight
2. He explains the importance of becoming like a child again
3. He puts His arms around the children
4. He blesses them

The result of His strategic insights into what is of real importance, is a new wonderment and a new perspective on the godlike qualities of children – the child as a kind of mirror image of admission to the Kingdom of God.
However, the moral of the story is even more profound. It deals with a much bigger issue, a much larger picture, namely the Kingdom of God. Jesus teaches them that the Kingdom does not belong to important adults only, but also to the most 'unimportant' human being (the child in the ancient world). In addition, this 'unimportant' child becomes the model for important people. Like a child trusts his/her parents for his/her livelihood, we have to trust God and depend on Him alone. In God's Kingdom there is no room for self-

complacent, important people. Unpretentious children understand this and they are the eternal example.

Jesus heals a paralysed man

Luke 5:17-26

17. One day while Jesus was teaching, some Pharisees and teachers of religious law were sitting nearby. (It seemed that these men showed up from every village in all Galilee and Judea, as well as from Jerusalem.) And the Lord's healing power was strongly with Jesus.

18. Some men came carrying a paralysed man on a sleeping mat. They tried to push through the crowd to Jesus.

19. But they couldn't reach him. So they went up to the roof, took off some tiles, and lowered the sick man down into the crowd, still on his mat, right in front of Jesus.

20. Seeing their faith, Jesus said to the man, *"Son, your sins are forgiven."*

21. *"Who does this man think he is?"* the Pharisees and teachers of religious law said to each other. *"This is blasphemy! Who but God can forgive sins?"*

22. Jesus knew what they were thinking, so he asked them, *"Why do you think this is blasphemy?"*

23. *"Is it easier to say, 'Your sins are forgiven' or 'Get up and walk?'"*

24. *"I will prove that I, the Son of Man, have the authority on earth to forgive sins."* Then Jesus turned to the paralysed man and said, *"Stand up, take your mat, and go on home, because you are healed!"*

25. And immediately, as everyone watched, the man jumped to his feet, picked up his mat, and went home praising God.

26. Everyone was gripped with great wonder and awe. And they praised God, saying over and over again, *"We have seen amazing things today."* (NLT)

Jesus' brain process (4)
Healing of the paralysed man

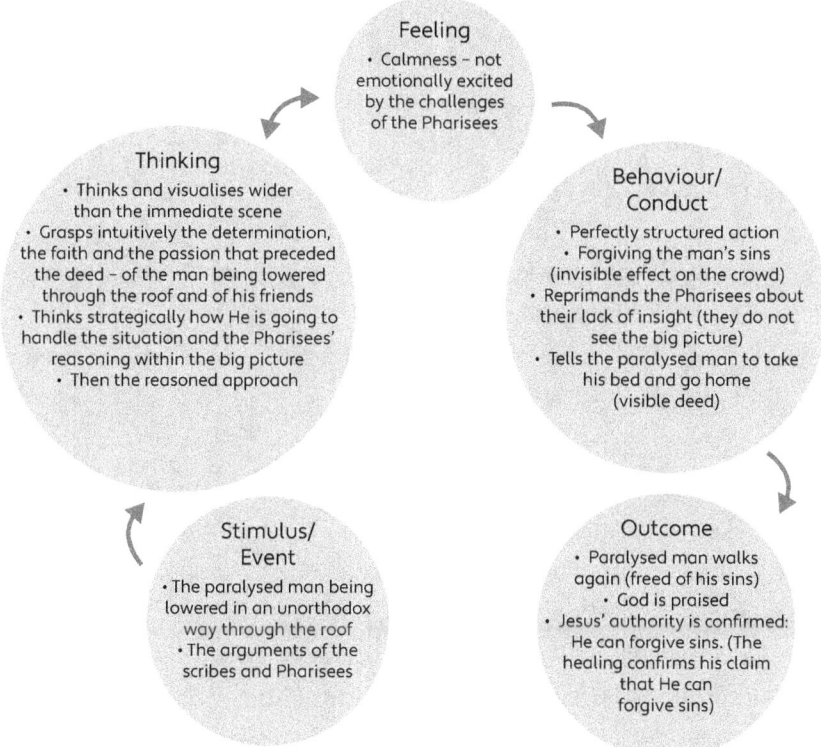

Healing of the paralysed man:
explanation

This exceptional event once again shows us Jesus as the perfect intuitive and strategic thinker. He finds himself in a situation where

He is surrounded by many people and we can imagine that there was a lot of activity and movement. His eye catches the man being lowered through the roof – a totally unique incident that unfolds within the context of larger events.

Once again Jesus grasps the uniqueness of the event unfolding – He immediately thinks innovatively; creates multiple ideas – something the onlookers do not do. Apparently they only see a man who is paralysed and who is being lowered into a room – a man who wants to be cured. In His brain, however, He sees:

- determination
- dedication
- a remarkable will
- a creative spirit (the ordinary way of trying to get through the crowd will not work, therefore an unorthodox, innovative way must be found to reach Him)
- trust that all these attempts will not be in vain – for ultimately he also desires forgiveness of his sins

Once again He supports this strategic right brain insight with a perfectly structured left brain action. From the invisible (to the crowd) *"Your sins are forgiven,"* there is a step-by-step clarification up to the visible, *"Stand up, take your mat, and go on home."*

In a situation like this with different role players, different motives and suddenly a dramatic incident that upsets the rhythm, Jesus proves himself to be the perfect strategist. Without the immediate structuring of all the events in His thinking and without a structured response, this incident could have had disastrous results. These events do not only show that Jesus can heal people, it also shows He can forgive sins – that He is God.

The question of taxes:

Luke 20:21-26

²¹· They said, *"Teacher, we know that you speak and teach what is right and are not influenced by what others think. You sincerely teach the ways of God."*

²²· Now tell us – is it right to pay taxes to the Roman government or not?"

²³· He saw through their trickery and said,

²⁴· *"Show me a Roman coin. Whose picture and title are stamped on it?"* *"Caesar's"* they replied.

²⁵. *"Well then,"* he said, *"Give to Caesar what belongs to him. But everything that belongs to God must be given to God."*

²⁶· So they failed to trap him in the presence of the people. Instead they were amazed by His answer, and they were silenced. (NLT)

Jesus' brain process (5)
The question of taxes

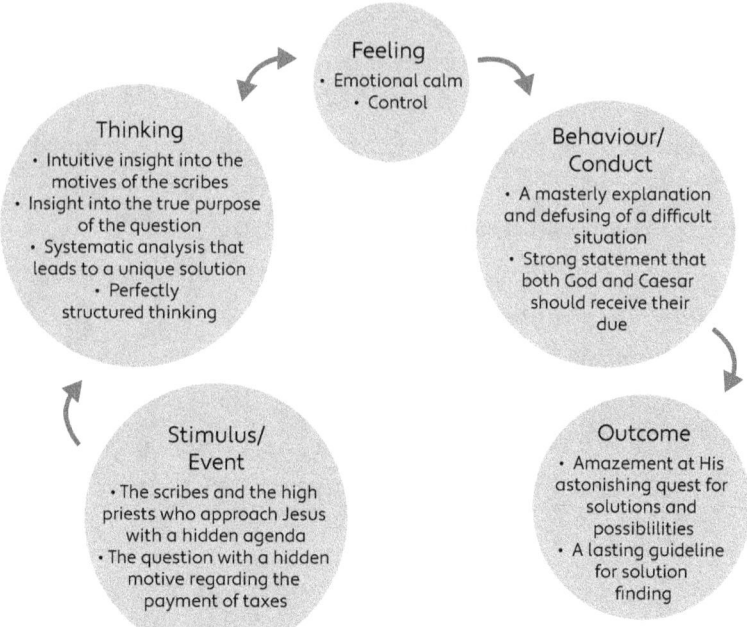

The question of taxes:
explanation

Once again Jesus is confronted, not with an ordinary situation, but with one that demands unusual, creative thinking. Because He immediately grasps the essence of the challenge, He can think of a strategy to generate a creative, meaningful solution.

This was a situation ready for conflict. The scribes, who obviously lacked the creativity for seeing the big picture, assumed that Jesus would give a clinically correct or wrong answer. It was a tricky question and they thought they would catch Jesus out. In their

rational thinking their kind of question had only two logical answers:
- Should Jesus say *"YES"*, He would lose the sympathy of the Jews
- Should He say *"NO"*, He would fall into disfavour with the Roman government

But Jesus' creative brain comes with an inclusive response – one so all-encompassing that it astounds His audience.

This event is indicative of many others where Jesus is confronted with an unusual problem. It is remarkable that He does not experience such situations as problematic.

His thinking immediately moves to solution finding. He does not dwell on what is negative about the circumstances, but once again, He is the strategic thinker par excellence. His vision is broader and more encompassing than that of the people around Him and He is able to solve conflict in a remarkable way – going way beyond the paradigms of His time.

What is also very clear is that He not only generates ideas about solutions; He also puts them into practice. The practical application always follows the creative ideas: *"Show me a Roman coin. Whose picture and title are stamped on it?"* And again: *"Give to Caesar what belongs to him. But everything that belongs to God must be given to God."*

The adulterous woman

John 8:1-11

1. Jesus returned to the mount of Olives, but early the next morning he was back again at the Temple.
2. A crowd soon gathered, and he sat down and taught them.

3. As he was speaking, the teachers of religious law and Pharisees brought a woman they had caught in the act of adultery. They put her in front of the crowd.

4. *"Teacher,"* they said to Jesus, *"this woman was caught in the very act of adultery."*

5. The law of Moses says to stone her. What do you say?

6. They were trying to trap him into saying something they could use against him, but Jesus stooped down and wrote in the dust with His finger.

7. They kept demanding an answer, so he stood up again and said, *"All right, stone her. But let those who have never sinned throw the first stones!"*

8. Then he stooped down again and wrote in the dust.

9. When the accusers heard this, they slipped away one by one, beginning with the oldest, until only Jesus was left in the middle of the crowd with the woman.

10. Then Jesus stood up again and said to her, *"Where are your accusers? Didn't even one of them condemn you?"*

11. *"No, Lord,"* she said. And Jesus said, *"Neither do I. Go and sin no more."* (NLT)

Jesus' brain process (6)
The adulterous woman

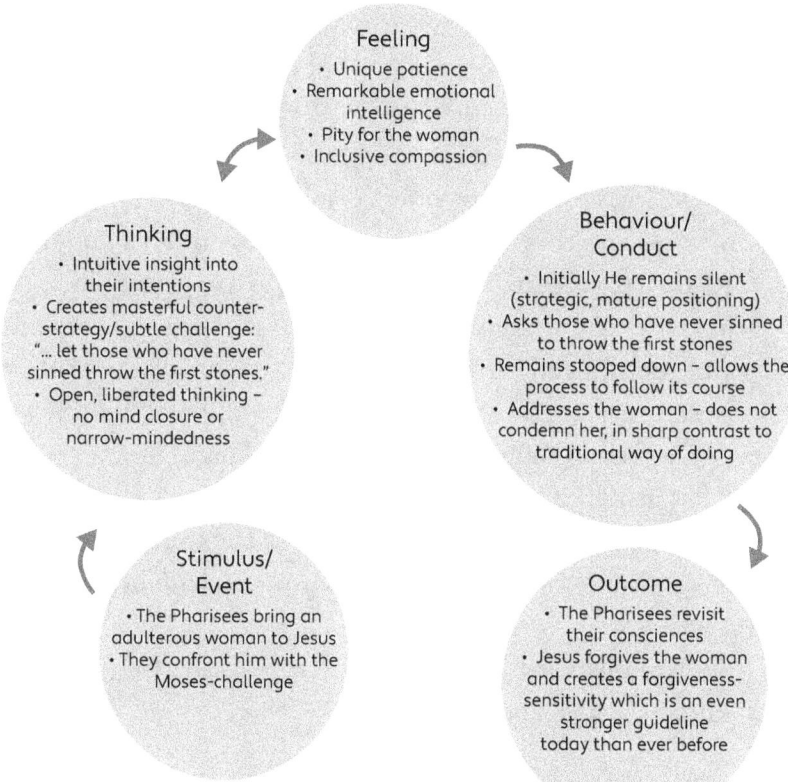

The adulterous woman:
explanation

This is once again a typical example of a sin that was committed, a transgression of Moses' law, and the traditional, rule-bound handling of the transgression versus Jesus' liberated, open-minded approach. The event that activates the brain processes is the scribes and Pharisees that bring an adulterous woman to Him. It is interesting that the

Pharisees do not ask for an immediate response. They explain the legal situation first and how to act according to Moses' law. But they do not quote Moses' law quite correctly – also to set a trap for Jesus. Lev. 20:10 says both the man and the woman should be killed. They caught the woman in the act, which implies that the man was also caught, but they bring only the woman to Him. Should Jesus say that she is to be stoned, they could say He does not know the law, for both have to be killed. (Note that under Roman law they cannot just kill as they please – and they do not want to!) On the other hand, should Jesus say, *"Let her go,"* they could say He approves of her sin.

Jesus, the wise strategist, does not react. He gives them ample time to put their 'legal' cards on the table – sins must be punished, the law says. Jesus clearly sees the big picture and His unique action is preceded by remarkably open, flexible thinking.

- He has insight into the deeper meaning of this specific incident
- Calmly, without openly condemning, He thinks creatively – and as always generates more than one possibility, answer or response
- Jesus' creative, open thinking leads to sensitive forgiveness and then 1 + 1 does not always equal 2.

The result of Jesus' resistance to closed thinking, is a model of forgiveness that has become stronger through the ages. It is as if this incident conclusively underlines the wisdom of Jesus. It is wisdom that follows a thinking process directed at creative solutions, where other people only see problems. This wisdom can only become holy when it is grounded on forgiveness: *"Let those who have never sinned throw the first stones."*

The Sermon on the Mount

Matt. 4:25; 5:1-12; 7:28-29

Matt 4:25

25. Large crowds followed him wherever he went – people from Galilee, the Ten Towns (the Decapolis), Jerusalem, from all over Judea, and from east of the Jordan River.

Matt 5:1-12

1. One day as the crowds were gathering, Jesus went up the mountainside with his disciples and sat down to teach them.
2. This is what he taught them:
3. *"God blesses those who realize their need for him* (Greek; the poor in spirit), *for the Kingdom of Heaven is given to them."*
4. God blesses those who mourn, for they will be comforted.
5. God blesses those who are gentle and lowly, for the whole earth will belong to them.
6. God blesses those who are hungry and thirsty for justice, for they will receive it in full.
7. God blesses those who are merciful, for they will be shown mercy.
8. God blesses those whose hearts are pure, for they will see God.
9. God blesses those who work for peace, for they will be called the children of God.
10. God blesses those who are persecuted because they live for God, for the Kingdom of Heaven is theirs.
11. God blesses you when you are mocked and persecuted and lied about because you are my followers.

12. *"Be happy about it! Be very glad! For a great reward awaits you in heaven. And remember the ancient prophets were persecuted too."*

Matt 7:28-29

28. After Jesus finished speaking, the crowds were amazed at his teaching,
29. for he taught as one who had real authority – quite unlike the teachers of religious law. (NLT)

Jesus' brain process (7)
The sermon on the mount

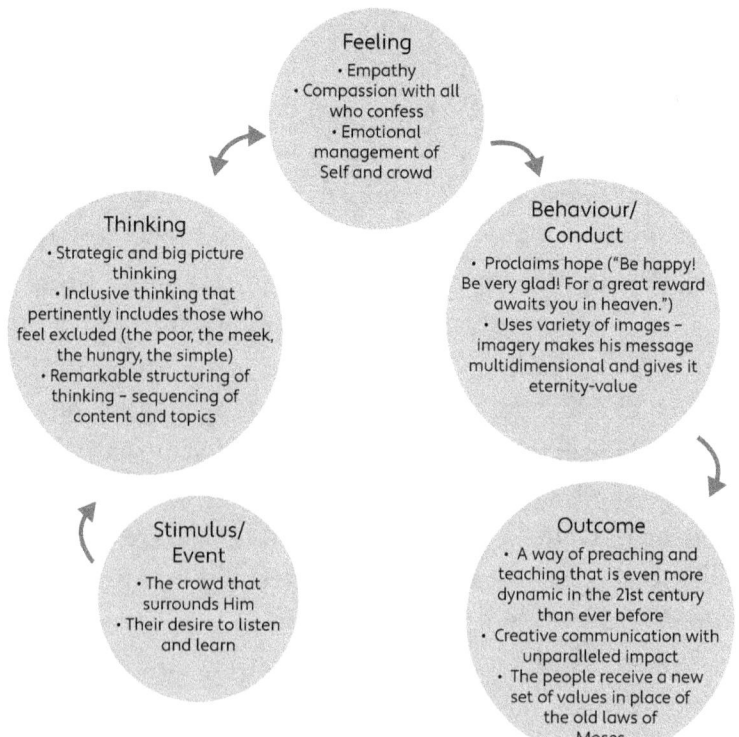

The sermon on the mount
explanation

During the Sermon on the Mount Jesus not only demonstrates His excellent teaching and communication skills, but also the remarkable way in which He can structure His thinking to make the greatest possible impact.

There is a huge crowd that would certainly include people from the total spectrum of society. They await His teaching and everyone certainly expects a special message.

Jesus has intuitive insight into the composition of the crowd. He knows there are learned people, rich people, people from a respected class and with social standing, who certainly have positive self-concepts and who feel good about themselves.

In contrast to these people He knows there are others who are poor, sick, from classes and spheres that do not command respect – people who probably doubt themselves or have low self-esteem. Jesus demonstrates a remarkable strategy – He pertinently includes everybody in His Sermon on the Mount. This inclusive approach has become the model for education, teaching and communication through the ages. Jesus includes everybody and today this methodology is more relevant than ever.

His strategic thinking, His empathic attitude and His innovative behaviour make Him the perfect role model:
- He is intuitively sensitive to the expectant crowd
- In His thinking He distinguishes group diversity
- He uses a form of imagery and creative language that eternalises the message and its impact
- He creates a future image of hope and excitement (*"For great awards await you in heaven"*)

He gives the people a set of values that will ensure happiness – an antipode to the old Law of Moses.

Jesus realises that a future without pull is sterile and meaningless. Here He sets guidelines regarding a vision – you must be able to visualise it and it must excite you. Unfortunately, few organisations in the past few centuries have shown interest in creating visions the way Jesus advocated. Visions are often created through rational thinking and in terms that can be evaluated concretely, instead of following Jesus' example of first creating feeling-oriented images in the thinking process and then to move to logic and structure.

When we examine every action of Jesus, as portrayed in the four Gospels, according to this model, we start discovering particular patterns that give us incredible insights into His thinking. It would take volume after volume to document each of His actions in this manner, but the objective of this book is to record the essence of our deductions and findings and not to elaborate on each event.

The brain processing of Jesus, the perfect human being, presents a model that is probably more significant in the 21st century than ever before. He is confronted with a variety of options for handling problems, relationships and challenges. Jesus faces His challenges with amazing creativity, and our research shows that this creativity seems to manifest in seven major thinking preferences.

1. Metaphor
2. Paradox
3. Intuition
4. Image streaming
5. System thinking
6. Out of the box thinking
7. Whole brain thinking (from abstract to logic)

Although there are other thinking strategies that Jesus continually uses, the ones that we single out appear to be more dominant and spontaneous. It becomes clear that Jesus holds up these thinking strategies as examples to us so that we can also think uniquely and innovatively about our situations.

At a time in history where the tempo and complexities of life are increasing dramatically and there are more challenges than ever, exceptional thinking simply cannot happen once in a while – it is a permanent demand the world makes on every person; a demand to take quantum leaps in our thinking: to keep on challenging the paradigms; to resist ordinary thinking and become mega creative thinkers.

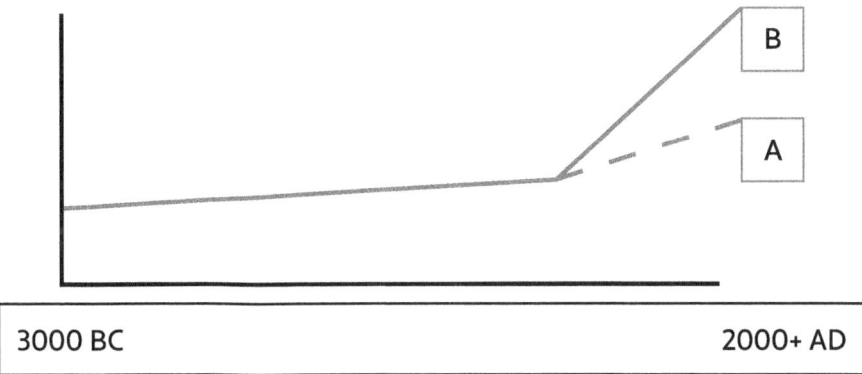

A major problem of the average person in the process person in the process of renewal and change, finds himself at A in a world that has already arrived at B. Generally speaking, it is not because most people are resistant to or negative about the quantum requirements of this century – the change and tempo towards A are much faster than in the past, and most people accept this. The tempo towards point B is, however, so much faster and more complex that even an accelerated tempo will have only limited success. We need to leap – and for this we need a new kind of creative ability – creative leaping skills.

Jesus continually soars in His thinking to B when circumstances challenge Him to do so. Our challenge is to function, like Jesus, comfortably at point B. He gives the guideline – a very clear guideline – on how to function with passion and zeal at point B. The main difference between the 20th and 21st century lies in the tempo and multiplicity: everything comes at us faster and from more directions. Jesus' Think-and-do Model offers us guidelines for finding possibilities and opportunities in spite of the exploding circumstances.

> *"Remember to welcome strangers in your homes. There were some Do not be conformed to this world, but be transformed by the renewal of your mind, that you may prove what the will of God is, what is good, acceptable and perfect."*
>
> **– Romans 12:2**

THREE

THE METAPHOR:
YOUR JOYFUL FOUNTAINS ARE WITHIN

In this chapter we want to:

- endorse the use of the metaphor as a powerful thinking technique
- illustrate Jesus' use of the metaphor
- pay tribute to Jesus as exponent of the metaphor for all times
- emphasise the value of metaphorical thinking in the 21st century

What is metaphorical thinking?

A common definition of metaphorical thinking is that it is either an implied or an explicitly stated comparison. It does two things simultaneously:
- it affords intellectual illumination
- it affords emotional excitement

The Oxford Advanced Learner's Dictionary (Oxford University Press, 1989) defines metaphor as follows:

Use of a word or phrase to indicate something different from (though related in some way to) the literal meaning.

Traditionally, in Linguistics and Theology a fine distinction is made between a metaphor and a simile. If an expression contains the comparative 'like' or 'as', e.g. 'as strong as an ox,' it is called a simile. Without the comparative 'like' or 'as', e.g. 'he is an ox', an image is created that provides endless new possibilities. The metaphor creates different new patterns which can result in unique illumination.

In this chapter we focus largely on Jesus' use of metaphor. It is one of His dominant thinking techniques that He applies excellently to transform situations, conflict and problems into unique solutions and possibilities. The metaphors Jesus uses so frequently, show a remarkably dynamic, creative power which inherently means new dimensions of thinking and language usage.

The remarkable power of the metaphor lies in the unique wealth of associations that can be created and may lead to original renewal and breakthroughs. As a result of its empathic nature the metaphor addresses the person directly – it is essentially a right brain experience:
- an image or picture is created in the brain (Right brain – imaging)
- it leads to a feeling of excitement (Right brain – emotional experience)

This metaphorical experience becomes a practical experience when the ideas become reality to the thinker (further interpretation by the left brain).

The metaphor remains one of the most powerful thinking

possibilities we have. When one starts connecting two different worlds and looks for meaning in the connection, new dimensions of insight and meaning are opened. When you compare one colleague (one world) to another (another world), you quickly notice characteristics like freedom, quick paradigm shifts and focus. In this way our thinking grows beyond narrow-mindedness and the metaphor becomes a road map giving direction to our insight and understanding.

Many intricate situations become more lucid when the metaphor is used to enhance understanding. The Old and the New Testament have a wealth of metaphors that are applied to simplify complicated situations. In Psalm 118:22 the metaphoric description is that of a stone which becomes a cornerstone – that which supports the building. The powerful metaphor of the cornerstone symbolises Christ and the builders, the Jews, who do not assign the most important stone its rightful place.

Jesus uses various forms of metaphoric thinking:
- to describe one thing in terms of another
- to give insight into a complicated situation
- to elevate and sanctify the experiences of people in a way that ordinary words and thoughts cannot achieve
- as an invitation to act (action follows listening)
- as an indisputable embodiment of His Divinity (He was not like God (comparison/simile); He was God (metaphor)

Jesus uses metaphors in His teachings to make His message effective beyond time and immediacy. These metaphors derive from daily life as ancient people experienced it, and that is what makes them so effective. Because they have a timeless quality, they have just as much impact on modern man.

A metaphor is not necessarily timeless. For example, if I say,

'Jesus is my motherboard,' the metaphor of 'motherboard' will probably not be effective for long, because technology changes so fast. But the metaphors Jesus used in His day have stood the test of time.

In John 8:12 He says, for example, *"I am the light of the world."* With this striking metaphor Jesus says that He has come to the world to dispel the darkness in which the people live.

In John 4 Jesus says to the Samaritan woman that He is the living water. Whoever drinks of this water will never be thirsty again. In the dry Middle East, water was not as plentiful as in many other countries. Thus water was associated with 'life'. So Jesus actually says that He gives us life. Nevertheless, though we live in a completely different part of the world, this metaphor remains relevant and meaningful.

Jesus not only tells people more about Himself through His metaphors, He also uses them when He talks about people as his followers. For example He says, *"You are the salt of the earth."* (Matt 5:13). He compares the permeating effect of salt to man's task on earth. Christians should be like salt. Their influence should enrich the entire world.

Jesus' metaphors

It is true that some of the metaphors Jesus used had far more impact in His own time than the same metaphor would have today. Therefore, in order to understand the metaphor properly, we need to have the same knowledge that His audience had. Yet, the spiritual power of Jesus' metaphors have, in a unique way, stood the test of time and space. Jesus' metaphors are timeless and still have a remarkable impact inside and outside the church environment today. Even after 2000 years we have no problem understanding them; they still create clear images in our minds and bring new insights.

Let us look at seven examples of metaphors Jesus uses:

1. Light

Jesus says, *"I am the light of the world."* (John 8:12)

In order to grasp the impact this metaphor had on Jesus' audience, we must first understand the ancient world. In the modern world we have so many street lights and lights in our houses that our nights are not very dark. However, if we are in a forest at night where no artificial light lights up the sky, we can form an idea of how intensely ancient people experienced darkness. Hence their fear of darkness, and there were many beliefs about demons and other evil spirits that roamed at night. To have a light in such darkness was a tremendous relief and comfort.

This is precisely what Jesus says. He says that without God we live in complete darkness. We have no refuge or future vision, and live in fear without any form of security. But Jesus came to humanity in this desolate situation and became our light.

With this striking metaphor Jesus says that He has come to the world to dispel the darkness in which humanity lives.

Metaphors have many possible applications. Although Jesus is our light, it does not prevent Him from saying that we should also be the light. In Matt 5:14 Jesus says,

"You are the light of the world. A city on a hill cannot be hidden. 15. Neither do people light a lamp and put it under a bowl. Instead, they put it on its stand and it gives light to everyone in the house." (NLT) And in verse 16, *"In the same way, let your light shine before men, that they may see your good deeds and praise your Father in heaven."*

With this metaphor Christ says that a believer should not just blend in with the world. Christians should be visible. Their lives must show the world that Christ does make a difference.

2. Salt

In the same chapter in Matthew (5:13) Jesus says:

"You are the salt of the earth. But what good is salt if it has lost its flavour? Can you make it useful again? It will be thrown out and trampled underfoot as worthless."(NLT)

In modern times we can easily argue that, scientifically speaking, sodium chloride cannot 'lose its flavour', therefore Jesus' metaphor is inaccurate. Once again we must realise that in ancient times the salt they used was not very pure. The salt from the lakes and rocks near the Dead Sea was of a poor quality and it was mixed with various other substances. Thus when salt was used in ancient times, a residue always remained. They could do nothing with it, because it had no salty flavour. It was thrown outside where people walked on it.

Thus Jesus' metaphors originate from the world in which He lives.

He compares the permeating function of salt to our task on earth. You only need to add a small quantity of salt to water, to make it taste salty. Christians should be like this. Their influence must enrich the entire world. But when believers become like the rest of the world and embrace its norms, they are 'flavourless' and useless.

3. Water

Jesus says to the Samaritan woman that He is living water:
In John 4:13 Jesus replied, *"People soon become thirsty again after drinking this water. 14. But the water I give them takes away their thirst altogether. It becomes a perpetual spring within them giving them eternal life."* (NLT)

In the dry Middle East water was scarce and often a rare commodity. Westerners in general have reasonably easy access to more than one water tap in their immediate environment. Because water was so scarce in the Middle East, it was very precious. When someone accidentally came across water it was a special treat and refreshment. Thus it was associated with life. When Jesus says He is our 'living water', He actually says that He gives us life. Nevertheless, even if we live in a totally different part of the world, this metaphor still succeeds in conveying its message effectively.

4. Rock

Jesus uses another well-known item from the Palestinian landscape when He refers to Peter as a 'rock'. In answer to Jesus' question, *"Who do you say I am?"* Peter replied, *"You are the Christ, the Son of the living God."* Then Jesus said, *"Blessed are you, Simon son of Jonah, for this was not revealed to you by man, but by my Father in heaven. And I tell you that you are Peter, and on this rock I will build my church, and all the gates of Hades (all the powers of hell) will not overcome it."* (Matt. 16:15 – 18)

A rock is something that exists very specifically in everybody's frame of reference. We all know that a rock is solid and cannot simply be pushed over or rolled away. Jesus says Peter is a rock. The effect of the metaphor is enhanced by the fact that the name 'Peter' actually means 'rock'. Why does Jesus call him a rock? The answer lies in what Peter says. Jesus asks how the disciples see Him, and Peter replies, *"You are the Christ, the Son of the living God."* This confession of faith would in centuries to come form the basis (the rock) of every Christian congregation. Nobody would ever be able to push over or destroy this confession. It stands as firm as a rock.

5. Door (or entrance)

In the NKJV we read in John 10:9 that Jesus said,
"I am the door. If anyone enters by Me, he will be saved, and will go in and out and find pasture."

This is, however, not a very accurate translation from the original Greek. Firstly, a sheepfold has no 'door'; it has a gate. But a door or a gate is something that bars your entrance. And this is not what Jesus does. He is not a door, but rather an 'opening' in which the door fits – He is the entrance! That is also how the New Translation puts it.

Sheep are always safe inside a fold and it may be dangerous outside it. It is the same with us. We have only one safe haven and that is the Kingdom of God – in other words, God's fold. By using the metaphor of the 'door' ('entrance'), Jesus succeeds in illustrating very clearly that the only way to get into the Kingdom of God is through Him. He is the entrance.

But what is meant by 'Kingdom of God'? Is it physically some place on earth or in heaven? No! The Kingdom of God is not just something that lies in the future. The term 'Kingdom of God' means that God is king of your life. It means He rules your life. Therefore we can already experience on earth what it means to be part of God's Kingdom. We do not have to wait till one day in heaven! And when Jesus is king of your life, you experience the feeling of safety a sheep has in the fold. Then you have so much security and freedom that you can *"go in and out and find pasture."* This means that you can experience life in abundance.

Even though this metaphor is derived from the life of a sheep farmer, its simplicity and effectiveness has given it universal appeal.

6. Bread

Jesus is also bread:
"I am the bread of life. No one who comes to me will ever be hungry again. Those who believe in me will never thirst."

In many countries of the world bread forms the staple diet. It was even more so in the ancient world. Many people used to be and are still dependent on bread for their survival. Thus Jesus teaches us in the Lord's Prayer to ask, *"Give us this day our daily bread."* Because bread is such an essential part of our daily lives, we must understand that 'bread' in the Lord's Prayer actually refers to food in a wider context. It should even be understood in a broader sense, namely that we ask God to take care of our entire existence. When we offer this prayer, we actually bring all our needs to Him and ask Him to provide for us fully.

We all need bread to sustain us. We can live on bread. Bread, therefore, implies life. When Jesus says (John 6:35) He is our bread, He means that He gives us life. He gives us true life –

eternal life. Thereby He promises that whoever comes to Him will never be hungry again.

Again it is easy for a modern person to identify fully with the meaning of this timeless metaphor. Jesus is an excellent teacher, a creative teacher, and by making use of metaphors He immortalises godly truths.

7. Way (path or road)

Throughout the ages there have been roads (paths, ways), and future generations will have roads (no matter what they will look like). All nations in all parts of the world know what a road is – it is universally known and therefore the road as symbol is universally understood . Jesus says He is the road (the way).

" I am the way, the truth and the life." (John 14:6). In order to understand this sentence correctly, we need to understand the principle first. In the Greek language when you combine two or three nouns with the conjunction 'and', it does not necessarily mean that these nouns are merely 'additions' and deal with two or three

different matters. For example, if I would say in English: *"I buy a book AND a pen"* it means I buy two separate items. It is not the same in Greek.

Often when one uses the word 'and' between two nouns in Greek, it does not mean that one is referring to two items. It deals with only ONE thing, but the second noun is used merely to describe the first.

Let us illustrate the principle in a practical way by referring to Jesus' statement: *"I am the way, the truth, and the life."* We read about three things, namely the way, the truth and the life, but in fact Jesus does not say three different things about Himself. He deals with one issue only. The three different nouns merely qualify one another. The focus is on the noun 'way'. Jesus says only He is the way (the road) to the Father. The noun 'truth' merely describes this way, namely that it is a 'true way'. The noun 'life,' in turn, describes the destination of this 'true way', namely (eternal) life. Thus, when Jesus says, *"I am the way, the truth and the life,"* He does not talk about THREE things, but only ONE, and that is: *"I am the true way (road) that has (eternal) life as its destination."* All other ways (roads) outside or without Jesus are dead ends. If one wants to enjoy eternal life, one has but one option – the way or road via Christ to the Father.

By making use of metaphors, as is very clear from these examples, Jesus creates a picture world for His listeners. Here we have proof of His creative thinking, vivid imagery and association, whole brain thinking; and that His thinking constantly focuses on solutions, on supplying answers and explanations, instead of being bogged down in problems.

Jesus proved that the use of the metaphor to emphasise truths, to answer questions in a simple manner, is a powerful thinking technique.

- Many businesses realise how effective metaphors can be as symbols of what they want to stand for. Examples of this are
  - the lion as symbol of power and leadership
  - the cheetah as symbol of speed and accuracy
  - the eagle as symbol of vision, respect and the ability to soar up high
- Teachers who are able to apply this technique will disclose a wonderful visual world to their students. Facts that are usually taught in a concrete (left brain) manner normally only have a short-term impact. When the same facts are taught with rich associations they are experienced in the right brain and it goes hand in hand with emotional experiences that students can recall later and that have a lasting effect. For example, students will have greater understanding for the close relation of plants and living creatures and their surroundings in the eco-system, if the tapestry metaphor is used: every thread which is pulled out will affect the whole, until eventually you are left with an empty frame.

But you do not really need to look for new metaphors to illustrate this technique. If we look at the implications of a few biblical metaphors, their relevance today is astounding.

The metaphors Jesus used to indicate how we should live and act have as much value today and even wider implications than when He was on earth.

The relevant question is, of course, how can metaphors like *"the light", "salt of the earth"*, etc., still contain messages for the people of today.

- Light as a metaphor today means something visible or familiar. All leaders of today (whether they are in the family, a company

or a country) can identify with this metaphor: the leader of the *"light"* has integrity, honesty and pure motives. It is also the symbol of transparency that we increasingly expect from our leaders today.
- Light also implies radiation. As parents, for example, we have a large responsibility as radiators. We should constantly ask ourselves how our children experience us. Are we positive, joyful (in spite of setbacks), or do we teach our children negative behaviour by setting a negative example?
- Light has always been the symbol of that which dispels darkness. This points to our mutual responsibility. Do other people experience us as lights that brighten up some of the darkness in their lives (by empathy, understanding, tolerance), or is it our irritation, sarcasm and discontentment that make their lives even darker.
- The salt metaphor has to do with taste, with our influence on the people we come into contact with. A positive influence springs from a joyful spirit and constructive words.
- The water metaphor remains the symbol of what quenches thirst, of what refreshes and revives. To us in the 21st century it implies inner qualities of strength that enable us to live contented, happy and grateful lives without constantly thirsting after something out of our reach.
- The rock metaphor is the symbol of sturdiness, firmness and is as fresh today as ever. It takes millions of years of wind, rain and sand to make a small hole in a rock. Yet how easily do we not crumble. A disappointment, a promotion that has not materialised, disobedient children, unfriendly people, a mother-in-law (or daughter-in-law) that is not your first choice, etc. – do you crumble? Remember that it is particularly in

rough weather conditions that the rock is put to the test.
- The entrance metaphor is the symbol of both place and action. The well-known writer, Stephen Covey, says: *"What a tragedy if we spend our whole life climbing to get to the top of the ladder, and when we get there we discover that it is leaning against a wrong wall."* Often this is the tragedy of modern people: they blindly force their way up the ladder of success without considering the final PLACE they want to arrive at, and whether it will really bring the joy they expect.
- Bread is also a metaphor for what we deserve or get as a reward. To be rewarded, praised and to get what we 'deserve', make us feel good. But the person who depends on these for his/her happiness, will definitely be disappointed quite often. We have to develop inner strengths so that we can appreciate rewards, but we should not expect them and definitely do not need them to retain our passion and joy in life.
- Way represents the manner of getting from one place to another, as well as the route and direction. Road thus becomes the metaphor for the visions and futures in life. As the environments around us change faster and faster, we have to realise that, just like a road, our visions will sometimes take unexpected turns. Often there are detours before we reach our destinations. Our visions for the 21st century must be flexible or we shall find ourselves in a cul-de-sac.
- Way (road) is also the symbol for a passage (making your way through something). It is a fact that life has many obstacles in store for us. The question is whether we shall be daunted by the first tree in our way, the river that floods the road, the apparently impenetrable forest, or whether the obstacles will inspire us to prove that we are pathfinders, pioneers!

The examples are legion – the potential to keep on applying Jesus' metaphors in the diverse challenges of our time is limitless.

Jesus' metaphors are universal and eternal because with this kind of image, seeing the picture in your mind, there are always possibilities for 'hitch-hiking' creatively, for elaborating and innovating so that the metaphor retains its lasting effectiveness.

> *To be around the beauty and colour of butterflies you have to nurture a lot of caterpillars.*

FOUR

PARADOX:
THE OPPOSITE OF THE TRUTH CAN BE THE TRUTH

In this chapter we want to:

- highlight the paradox as an unusual, challenging and extremely advanced approach to thinking
- try to discover the essence of Jesus' paradoxical thinking
- place the accent on Jesus' paradoxes as strategies which challenged the paradigms of His time
- point out the relevance of His paradoxes to the 21st century

The following definition of paradox is taken from the Oxford Advanced Learner's Dictionary:
1. statement that seems to be absurd or contradictory but is or may be true: 'More haste less speed,' is a well-known paradox.
2. person, thing or situation displaying contradictory features.

Paul uses many paradoxes in 2 Corinthians 6:10 where he says they are *"sorrowful, yet always rejoicing; poor, yet making many rich; having nothing, and yet possessing everything."*

Paradox requires a special level of understanding and is meant to be qualified and explained. The purpose of paradox is to challenge conventional ways of thinking and to come up with alternative ideas. We all have an element of the absurd in us and the paradox asks us to juggle our thoughts and view the situation from a whole new perspective.

Furthermore, the paradox requires that our thinking moves in leaps and bounds in order to link worlds and contents which have no apparent connection. But it is precisely this practically impossible leap which can elevate our thinking and insights to extraordinary levels. We put into process a new way of looking and acting when we start making use of paradoxical connections.

The demands that the paradox makes on us is that our thinking needs to handle two diverse images or portrayals simultaneously. It is only when we succeed in associating one concept with the other that new, exceptional insights are born. To be able to grasp the paradox, means that we must make *"forced connections"*. Once the association starts making sense it can lead to remarkable insights – a new illumination which can result in creative breakthroughs. Today the paradox is regarded as one of the most powerful thinking techniques in leading the way to exceptional thinking – looking past the ordinary and the mundane and seeing solutions which seemed impossible before.

Jesus is the ultimate in using the paradox. He tells you if you want life, you will lose it; the person who is last will be first, and the person who wants to be the most important among you, must be your servant. Therefore it is essential that He should introduce us to the deeper dimensions of paradox, for as Paul says,

> *If you think you are wise by this world's standards, you will have to become a fool so you can become wise by God's standards.*
>
> **— 1 Corinthians 3:18**

Jesus the paradox thinker

Let us look in more detail at seven examples of paradox that Jesus used in His teachings:

1. *Whoever finds his life will lose it, and whoever loses his life for my sake will find it.* (Matt 10:39)

Here Jesus uses paradox very interestingly: He first puts it positively, then He turns the paradox around and puts it negatively. It was a popular rhetorical technique in the ancient world to state important truths both positively and negatively. For example, Paul says in 1 Tim. 2:7, *"I am telling the truth – I am not lying…"* (first positive then negative). John the Evangelist (1:3) writes, *"Through him all things were made; without him nothing was made…"* (once again these two important truths are presented both positively and negatively).

The above-quoted paradox contains an exceptional truth: that is why Jesus puts it so forcefully. But at first glance the meaning is not so obvious – typical of the paradox. However, when we really start thinking it through, it starts making exceptional sense.

Let us start with the first paradox: *"Whoever finds his life will lose it"*. Many people feel that they really start living when they participate in everything the world has to offer: financial security, fame, success, pleasure, power, popularity, and so forth. So one can easily believe that when one has attained many of these worldly things, one can really live – that one has *"found life"*. But when these matters are carefully considered, this kind of life seems empty. What the world offers, may easily become so important that a person builds his/her entire life on it, and forfeits eternal life. That is why Jesus says that a person with such misplaced values can *"lose his life"*.

But then He turns the paradox around: *"Whoever loses his life for my sake will find it."* Jesus is saying that the person who does not always put his/her own interests first, but chooses Christ, is the one who will experience the true sense and meaning of life.

The 'advantage' of such an attitude is not only in eternal life here-after, but it can also add more meaning to one's life on earth here and now. But *"to lose your life"* need not only be taken up figuratively, as if it merely refers to sacrificing and forfeiting your own interests. Possibly Jesus also refers to the reality of the church in earlier times where many Christians literally lost their lives because they had chosen Christ. With this paradox Jesus reassures His followers that they will never choose Him in vain. In the end they can rest assured that they will live with God the Father forever.

2. *See to it, then, that the light within you is not darkness.* (Luke 11:35)

This is impossible! Light cannot be darkness! Yet Jesus warns us to be careful that the light within us is not darkness. To understand this paradox better, it is necessary to look at the preceding verse as well (verse 34): *"Your eye is the lamp of your body. When your eyes are good, your whole body also is full of light. But when they are bad your whole body also is full of darkness."*

People of ancient times did not have the same biological

knowledge that we have. It was believed that your eye sent out rays of light towards the object you looked at. This light merged with the light of the object and was then reflected back to your eye, which in turn sent it inside your body. Should you then look with a bad eye at things around you, your whole body would be dark. The term, bad eye, does not refer to bad eyesight, but figuratively to one without light. One looks with a 'bad eye' at something when, for example, one looks at the world around one with jealousy and envy. It has a negative effect on the way one experiences people and things around one. It also robs one of the positive joy of life. In such a case the light inside you (that your eye radiates) is pitch-dark. However, when you allow the Good News of Jesus to light up your whole being, you will indeed be spiritually illuminated. Then you will be enabled to act according to these 'enlightened' insights.

3. *Blessed are those who mourn …* (Matt 5:4)

This verse may at first not look like a true paradox. The reason is that it is not translated correctly. We often use the word 'blessed' in the sense of 'rich' or 'favoured'. For example we would say a person is 'blessed' with many talents. But this is not what the Greek word makarios means. Makarios rather means 'happy.'

In Matthew 5 Jesus discusses what it is that really makes people 'happy'. The criteria He uses are in direct contrast to those that the world as we know it would use to describe happiness. The world thinks you are happy when you laugh, when you seem glad and cheerful. But then Jesus uses a paradox and says, 'Oh no. Do you know who is truly happy? Those who are sad, those who mourn.' When you read His words for the first time they do not make sense at all. But then Jesus supplies the reason: '..for they will be comforted.'

The Greek construction used here implies that God is the one who comforts. It is not just anybody, your neighbours or friends who will comfort you when you mourn, God himself will be your comforter.

The translation of this verse in the Good News Bible is much more appropriate: 'Happy are those who mourn; God will comfort them.' That is why every believer who is sad can be happy as well, for he/she knows that God, with His comforting hand, is right next to him/her.

4. *But many who are first will be last, and many who are last will be first.* (Matt 19:30)

Again Jesus uses a paradox when He says, *"But many who are first will be last."* Then He turns the paradox completely around to add, *"… and many who are last will be first."* Exactly 16 verses later (Matt 20:16) He turns the whole paradox around once again when He says,
 "So the last will be first, and the first will be last."

Again we have to consider this paradox carefully before we can understand its meaning. The first mistake we make is to think that 'first' and 'last' refer to time. These terms should much rather be translated as *"most important"* and *"least important."* Jesus says that in God's Kingdom the values as we know them on earth will be reversed completely. All the human positions (ranks, classes, degrees and titles) that we know in society will count for nothing in the hereafter. God applies different norms. God chooses His people according to His all-powerful grace and does not take into account what we have achieved on earth.

5. *Instead, the greatest among you should be like the youngest, and the one who rules like the one who serves.* (Luke 22:26)

The terms *"greatest"* and *"youngest"* in this paradox have nothing to do with age. A child had absolutely no status in the ancient world.

In contrast, the elderly enjoyed much status. Like in the previous paradox we discussed, this one also refers to people who have status and people who do not, i.e. *"important"* and *"unimportant"* people.

Furthermore, this paradox about the *"greatest"* and the *"youngest"* is repeated in the parallel paradox about the *"one who rules"* and the *"one who serves"*.

But contrary to the third paradox (Matt. 19:30) discussed above, this one does not only refer to the status people will have in heaven as opposed to the status they enjoy on earth: it refers primarily to the attitude with which the leader of believers executes his/her task. It should never bear a trace of pride or vanity. Jesus asks that leaders and other *"important"* people who have status, should execute their tasks in all humility. In this regard Jesus Himself is the perfect model for His followers.

6.   *Give, and it will be given to you.* (Luke 6:38)

At a first reading these words do not make sense. It is obvious that when you give, you do not receive. The question that follows automatically is: who is going to give something back to you after you have given first? Does this verse refer to other people? The Greek construction of this Biblical verse shows clearly that God is the one who gives us something in return. The translation in the Good News Bible is very clear: *"Give to others, and God will give to you."*

Furthermore, Jesus uses a beautiful image to indicate how abundantly God gives of His goodness to us. Jesus says that God will give us, *"A good measure, pressed down, shaken together and running over."* (Luke 6:8) The image used here is taken from the world of the farmer. When a farmer had to measure wheat, he poured it into a bucket. But when God takes a measuring bucket to *"measure out"* His goodness to us, He presses the contents in firmly, shakes it and fills it to the brim. With this image Jesus shows us how abundantly God measures out His goodness to us.

7. *I tell you that this man, rather than the other, went home justified before God. For everyone who exalts himself will be humbled, and he who humbles himself will be exalted.* (Luke 18:14)

The paradoxes Jesus uses cannot always be expressed in a single sentence only. Sometimes a paradox covers a much wider field. The events themselves can be paradoxical. For example, when Jesus tells the parable of the tax collector and the Pharisees (Luke 18:14), He concludes with a paradoxical statement. Yet one only grasps the paradox when one considers the whole story: Jesus says that a Pharisee and a tax collector prayed at the temple. The Pharisee prayed as follows: *"God, I thank you that I am not like other men – robbers, evildoers, adulterers – or even like this tax collector. I fast twice a week and give a tenth of all I get."* In contrast, the tax collector's simple prayer was, *"God, have mercy on me, a sinner."*

The Pharisee undoubtedly lived an exemplary life. He obeyed all the religious laws of the time, and the Jews knew it. One can almost say the Pharisee was a perfect example of the devoted churchgoer of his time. In sharp contrast, the tax collectors were known to be corrupt. The whole town knew that they were a bunch of crooks. Yet Jesus says emphatically, *"I tell you that this man (the bad tax collector), rather than the other (the Pharisee), went home justified by God."* Jesus' paradoxical statement must have shocked His audience. It goes against all logic. Does Jesus mean we have to start committing sins, like the tax collector, so that we can be saved? Does it count against us if we live a good, clean life like the Pharisee?

However, when we analyse the parable in more detail and begin to understand the essence of the paradox, we realise that the tax collector noticed something about God that the Pharisee missed. The Pharisee thought God rewarded one for one's (good) deeds, while the tax collector sensed that God was love and that He had compassion for human beings. The tax collector knew he had nothing to boast about before God – he could only rely on the mercy of God.

For this reason Jesus says, *"I tell you that this man (the bad tax collector), rather than the other (the Pharisee), went home justified by God."* And then Jesus adds another paradoxical statement: *"..everyone who exalts himself will be humbled and everyone who humbles himself will be exalted."*

Jesus used the paradox to challenge the thinking of His listeners, to answer questions interestingly and uniquely, to address issues and teach lessons.

- the fact that the paradox aims at challenging conventional thinking and stimulating the brain to generate alternative ideas, makes it an essential tool in our rapidly changing world. Leaders, parents and businesses who do not shift paradigms regularly, will lag behind. Expressions like the following are examples of paradoxes that can serve as stimuli for our *"out of the box"* thinking:
  - *"tough love"*
  - *"sometimes we have to destroy to create"*
  - *"look internally for external perspective"*
- today we play on playing fields that were unknown only a few years ago. To be successful players we have to develop

our thinking to extraordinary levels. The paradox opens new worlds of thinking because we suddenly see connections between contents that seemed impossible earlier on. In this way many new and successful products and businesses originated, like-
   - the cordless telephone
   - fast foods
   - sugar-free sweeteners
   - ice-tea
   - alcohol-free beer (cholesterol-free oil)
- Paradoxes bring new insights when we have to handle two opposite poles. Old beliefs are confronted and lead to renewal. The following paradoxes are examples of such insights:
   - success is a moving target
   - yesterday's innovation is today's stagnation
   - in the turbulent, unstable environment of the 21st century you have to be the eye of the storm

> *"What we want, is to see the child in pursuit of knowledge, and not knowledge in pursuit of the child."*
>
> **– George Bernard Shaw**

FIVE

INTUITION –
TO KNOW BEFORE YOU KNOW

In this chapter we want to:

- illustrate the meaning and importance of intuition in our lives
- highlight and explain Jesus' use of intuition
- endorse intuition as an essential element of the thinking process

The Oxford Advanced Learner's Dictionary gives the following definition of intuition:
1. Power of understanding things (e.g. a situation, somebody's feelings) immediately, without the need for conscious reasoning or study
2. Piece of knowledge gained by this power

Webster's Desk Dictionary defines it as:
1. Direct perception of truth or fact, independent of any reasoning process
2. Keen and quick insight

Intuition is the ability we all have to know something directly without an analytical process. This kind of information that one knows intuitively, can be a feeling that one gets about something or somebody, or some specific knowledge that one develops about something concrete (e.g. that, if you make an offer on that house, it will be right on target and clinch the sale).

When one makes a decision based only on analytical, logical and rational processes, the decision-making process is founded on today and yesterday's information. Intuition is, in fact, non-analytical information and is exclusively a right brain process that adds unique dimensions to the thinking processes of the left brain.

During the intuitive process data is received without your knowing where it comes from. Once these internal processes are acknowledged and exercised and then combined with the processes of the left brain, like structuring, organising, rationalising and analysing, unique enlightenment is possible. Decisions that stem from this combined process generally show deeper insight and vision.

For many people intuition is a picture-experience; to see the big picture of the situation in one moment. Logical processes have not preceded this experience, and the big picture experience brings remarkable enlightenment. Other people experience intuition as a kind of 'inner voice' that talks to them, and a feeling of excitement accompanies these seeing and hearing experiences.

Although intuitive knowledge often has to do with things, it mostly concerns people. To appoint a new staff member from a short list of candidates, who all seem equally capable, is very difficult.

Mostly the concrete information about them does not tell the full story. With finely developed intuition, combined with factual data, a much more accurate assessment can be made. A parent's knowledge, without facts, that her child is struggling with a problem, or a manager who makes a business decision before she has all the details (and immediately knows it is the right decision), are examples of knowledge that has been directly provided by the process of intuition.

Unfortunately, especially the 20th century world of industry, business and education virtually excluded intuition as an important part of the thinking process. It was generally considered something irrational that did not deserve a place in decision-making, planning and creating futures. Our corporative, educational and even congregational worlds were managed by means of exact, logical and rational thinking. The intuitive powers of human beings were already established during Creation and the modern world will be adamant that we develop respect and openness towards the role of intuition in every aspect of our lives.

The more we acknowledge the important function of intuition in our homes, schools and businesses, the more we shall develop the confidence to depend on it when circumstances demand it from us. Once again Jesus set the remarkable example in His spontaneous use of intuitive thinking when circumstances necessitated it.

Biblical examples:

Jesus unquestionably had the ability to know and understand intuitively. One could certainly speculate for a long time about the origin of this ability. Some people will argue that Jesus knew certain things simply because He was also God. But then we have to remember that Jesus was at the same time also human and because He was human He was not given to know everything God knew. In a certain sense it restricted His Godliness. For example, Jesus says in Mark 13:32 about His second coming:

> *"No one knows about that day or hour, not even the angels in heaven, nor the Son, but only the Father."*

Others will argue that it was God or the Holy Spirit that gave Jesus certain information and that enabled Him simply to know certain things about people. But even the Bible is not always explicit about how Jesus knew. Yet it is clear that Jesus often could judge a situation or people accurately without His decision being based on logical or rational thinking.

Jesus washes His disciples' feet

(John 13:1-17)

Jesus knew His disciples very well. Without anyone telling Him about Judas, He knew Judas would be the one to betray Him. In John 13 we read that Jesus washes His disciples' feet. Usually it is the work of slaves. But Jesus wants to teach His disciples an important lesson. He sets them an example of how to be of service to one another. Initially Peter refuses that Jesus washes his feet. Peter does not grasp what Jesus means when He says to him that if He (Jesus) does not wash his (Peter's) feet, he will have no part of Him. This is why Peter wants Jesus to wash his hands and face as well. But Jesus replies,

"A person who has had a bath needs only to wash his feet, his whole body is clean. And you are clean, though not every one of you." (John 13:10) Then the Evangelist John adds, *"For he knew who was going to betray him, and that is why he said not everyone was clean."* (John 13:12)

It is also significant to note that the story unfolds during a meal. A meal in those days (like today) was an important social function characterised by great intimacy. You dine with people you share a special social bond with. For the same reason one feels uncomfortable when one sits in a restaurant and a stranger comes to sit at one's table and eats his food. Jesus enjoys a special moment of intimacy with His disciples, but in spite of the intimacy He knows that everything is not what it appears to be on the surface. He knows Judas will betray Him. We read in John 6:64, *"For Jesus had known from the beginning which of them did not believe and who would betray him."* Thus Jesus is not caught unawares when Judas comes up to him in the Garden of Gethsemane, and greets Him with a friendly, *"Good morning, Rabbi,"* and kisses Him. Jesus replies, *"Friend, do what you came for."*

The question of paying taxes

(Mark 12:13-17)

We read in Mark 12:13-17 that a few Pharisees come to Jesus. They say a few flattering things about Him, and then ask, *"Is it right to pay taxes to Caesar or not? Should we pay, or shouldn't we pay?"* Despite their flattery Jesus sees through their hypocrisy (verse 14). Mark says: *"But Jesus knew their hypocrisy."*

Jesus just knows these men are not sincere. He knows they have come to Him with a trick question. The ordinary people are averse to paying taxes to the Roman authorities because they believe they should only be subservient to God. The Pharisees know that if Jesus says they must pay the taxes He will lose support from the people. They also know that if He says they must not pay, He will land in great trouble with the Romans. But because Jesus intuitively knows the Pharisees' plan, He succeeds magnificently in gaining the creative edge. He simply answers, *"Give to Caesar what is Caesar's and to God what is God's"*.

The disciples argue about who is the most important

(Mark 9:33-37)

When Jesus and His disciples arrive at a house in Capernaum, He asks them what they were talking about along the road. They do not answer Him, because they were in fact arguing with one another about who is the most important. But they do not have to tell Jesus what they talked about. He knows exactly what it was all about.

Therefore He sits down and calls His disciples to Him. Then He teaches them a new value system: In contrast to people of the world they should rather be concerned about those who are not important in the eyes of the world. Then He calls a small child to Him and lets him stand among them. Then He illustrates precisely what He means – it is not the most important people who count. Much rather should we pay attention to the least important. By having summed up and understood their behaviour precisely, without having been told by anyone, He can now teach His disciples important religious values.

Believers and unbelievers among disciples

(John 6:60-71)

Jesus' conduct and teaching drew many people to Him. But soon they started to realise that the implications of Jesus' teachings were that they should be prepared to sacrifice, like Jesus, their entire lives. They were not ready for this, and would no longer stay with Him.

They started complaining and going home. We read in John 6:60, *"On hearing it, many of his disciples said, 'This is a hard teaching. Who can accept it?'"*

In the next verse (6:61) we read, *"Jesus knew within himself that his disciples were complaining, so he said to them, 'Does this offend you?'"*(NLT) Through His godly insight Jesus knew the disciples were grumbling. It gave Him the opportunity to take the matter up with them and have an in-depth discussion about what it really meant to be His follower.

The fact that Jesus time and again demonstrates His *"gut-feeling"* – this insight into the thinking and feeling of His followers, gives Him a tremendous advantage. His evaluation of His disciples' questions is not always based on logic and rational thinking, Through intuition, combined with godly insight, He is able to identify the true essence of every situation.

The yeast of the Pharisees and the Sadducees

(Matthew 16:5-12)

In this part Jesus warns His disciples against the teachings of the Pharisees. He uses an image (metaphor) and says they have to beware of the yeast of the Pharisees and the Sadducees. Thereby He means they must be cautious about the influence these people have. But the disciples' immediate interpretation is that Jesus is hinting that they have not brought bread. They grumble to one another about it. Then we read in verse 8: *"Jesus knew what they were thinking, so he said, 'You of little faith, why are you talking among yourselves about having no bread?'"*

Jesus immediately knew that His disciples were grumbling and what they were talking about among themselves. That offered Him the opportunity of correcting their distorted thinking immediately.

The fact that Jesus instantly realised that they misinterpreted His remark, enabled Him to put things into perspective for them.

The man with the deformed hand

(Luke 6:6-11)

One Sabbath Jesus goes into the synagogue again. There is a man with a deformed right hand. The scribes and the Pharisees watch Jesus closely to see if He will heal the man on the Sabbath. Then we read the interesting information in verse 8: *"But Jesus knew what they were thinking and said to the man with the shriveled hand, 'Get up and stand in front of everyone.' So he got up and stood there."* Before anyone could say anything, Jesus confronted them with the question, *"I ask you, which is lawful on the Sabbath: to do good or to do evil, to save life or to destroy it?"*

Jesus knew exactly what went on in the minds of the scribes and the Pharisees. Because their warped views and ideas were so very clear to him He was able to strategise a new and meaningful framework for them in which to assess the miracle of His healing.

Jesus heals a paralysed man

(Matthew 9:1-8)

The people bring a paralysed man who is bedridden to Jesus. Jesus says to Him, *"Take heart, son; your sins are forgiven."* Then we read in verse 3: *"At this some of the teachers of the law said to themselves, 'This fellow is blaspheming!'""This man talks like God!"* NLT). In the next verse we read these significant words, *"Jesus knew what they were thinking, so he said to them, 'Why are you thinking such evil thoughts?'"* In the rest of the story we read how Jesus explains to them that He, as the Son of God, does have the authority to forgive sins on earth. Again Jesus is right on target in His teaching because He knows exactly what they are hiding in their hearts.

In conclusion

(Luke 6:6-11)

It is still difficult to know how Jesus, in the above-mentioned examples, secured some of His information. Did He simply intuitively feel certain things because He was so creative and open-minded, or did He know it on the grounds of His godly nature? There are indeed examples where Jesus shows He has premonitions or foreknowledge that cannot be ascribed merely to intuition. In John 1:45 Philip invites Nathanael to accompany him to Jesus. When Jesus sees Nathanael coming towards Him, He says of him, *"Here is a true Israelite, in whom there is nothing false."* (verse 47) When Nathanael asks from where Jesus knows him, Jesus replies, *"I saw you while you were still under the fig tree before Philip called you."* Here Jesus reveals superhuman and supernatural knowledge indeed.

In John 4 Jesus is in conversation with the Samaritan woman. At one stage He says to her, *"Go, call your husband and come back."* She answers that she has no husband. Jesus' amazing answer is, *"You are right when you say you have no husband. The fact is, you have had five husbands, and the man you now have is not your husband. What you have said is quite true."* (verse 17-18) Once again Jesus reveals remarkable, godly foreknowledge.

We must admit that there are clear examples in the Bible where Jesus could have known certain things only on the grounds of His godly nature. But some of the examples we discussed above can be ascribed to intuition and observation. We can assume that the latter characteristic could also be part of Jesus' human nature because He was after all also completely human (without denying thereby His godly characteristics and insight). Nevertheless, no matter how Jesus gained all this knowledge, it enabled Him to see the big picture of a situation in one moment. It is also clear that His decisions and behaviour were not based on precise, logical, and rational thinking only. His foreknowledge and often immediate, spontaneous analysis and grasp of the situation as well as of the people around Him, enabled Him to make fast, effective decisions.

In this century we cannot simply expand on information, facts and decisions of the past, and then apply it as the basis for today. Life changes so drastically that many of these logical outcomes no longer count. Intuition (feeling, knowing, often without logic) has an increasingly important role to play.

- In our relationships with others, intuition plays a critical part. That little voice that tells you rather to keep quiet, rather to take up the matter at a later stage, can prevent great damage to a relationship. The finer we develop our intuition about correct behaviour at the right place and at the right time, the wiser we as human beings will become.
- Intuition has an important part to play in emotional intelligence. I develop my emotional intelligence when I start *"feeling"* that something is wrong with someone, without concrete proof, and when I ask the correct empathic questions and thereby lead others to understand their own emotions better.
- When certain situations or people make us feel uncomfortable, it is a sure sign that our intuition alarm is going off and

- that we should do something about it. Thus we can avoid uncomfortable, even dangerous situations.
- It is also a fact that intuition has its place in the boardroom and business world. More and more successful businessmen and entrepreneurs state that it is their *"gut feel"*, that inexplicable, inner road sign, that helps them make business decisions that result in great profit. Yes, certainly facts and and analysis of the concrete are still essential, but the role of 'inner knowledge that it will work' has become more important.
- When new positions have to be filled, when there is the choice between different offers or the choice of a spouse, etc., intuitive decisions may often mean the difference between a nightmare relationship or that 'once in a lifetime' choice.

> *It is intuitive sensitivity that transforms the technician into an artist.*
>
> **– Hebrews 12:2**

Dr Kobus Neethling | Prof Hennie Stander | Dr Raché Rutherford

SIX

IMAGE STREAMING –
TO SEE THE WORLD IN A GRAIN OF SAND AND HEAVEN IN THE YELLOW OF THE SUNFLOWER

In this chapter we want to:

- explain the process of image streaming
- underline the importance of image streaming in creating new ideas, breakthrough insights and creativity
- highlight Jesus' continual use of image streaming to handle situations and people as one of His most important thinking preferences

The concept *"Image Streaming"* was developed in the last quarter of the 20th century. Creativity experts like Win Wenger and Richard Poe made this concept popular in their training programmes and publications (The Einstein Factor 1996, and Discovering the Obvious 1999). However, already as early as in 1953, Alex F. Osborn in his Applied Imagination: Principles and Procedures of Creative Problem Solving, underlined in different terms the importance of image streaming in the creative process. Mihaly Csikszentmihalyi in his *Flow: The Psychology of Optimal Experience* (1990) made a further important contribution to illustrate the creation and flow of creative images in the brain as a prerequisite for genial thinking.

Although the concept of 'image streaming' is relatively new, the process has existed since the beginning of Creation. When you describe a situation or object (right in front of your eyes or of which you have a picture in your imagination) more and more detail and different images start to appear. One of the most effective ways to keep creating a constant stream of images is to keep talking about them; for example telling a person about the images that you see or that you are creating in your mind. The more sensory your description, the more powerful the effect which is achieved.

Through exercising and repetition of these thinking skills one becomes more spontaneous in the use of image streaming. This thinking technique can be developed to exceptional heights so that the pictures one creates in one's brain later start making spontaneous connections and become a constant flow.

The most important historical breakthroughs probably originated in image streaming. Six centuries ago Leonardo da Vinci wrote in his Notebooks that, sometimes when one looks at a blotch on a wall, or at the clouds, or at ashes of a fire, other pictures start forming in the mind and from these stimuli new ideas are created. Furthermore he suggested that the hundreds of smaller details start taking on a shape of their own. In this way his remarkable works of art like the Mona Lisa and The Last Supper gained eternal value.

Einstein's famous words, *"We don't need more knowledge, we need more imagination,"* were a direct reference to image streaming and his own breakthroughs came as a result of this insight. His Relativity Theory, which virtually changed the direction of physics, did not originate, in the first place, as a result of mathematical calculations, but almost in an unexpected manner while he was daydreaming.

In his imagination he saw himself running along a sunbeam at the speed of light. This image gave rise to a series of other images in his mind – in contrast to most adults who would immediately ignore or reject such *"absurd"* images. These images played around in his brain and years later he saw himself on the front end of a ray of light, holding a mirror to his face. The question he asked himself was whether one could see one's face in that mirror while travelling at the speed of light. The answer from classical physics was no, because the light that left your face had to move faster than light to reach the mirror. Einstein, however, rejected the traditional answer from physics. Initially he had no proof, but the images in his brain seemed right and felt right. Years later he started testing the series of images mathematically and he created theories that changed the world.

Breakthroughs are not the result of logical thinking, although the final creation or product functions within logical structures. The New Testament bears witness of remarkable examples of image streaming.

Examples from the Bible

Although the concept 'image streaming' is very new, the process itself is not. Jesus and others before Him applied it. But before we look in more detail at a few examples of 'image streaming' in Jesus' thinking, it is important to remember that we do not have a verbatim report on His actions and teachings. The Evangelists were not writers in the true sense of the word. They were more like 'editors' of a newspaper. Therefore they did not narrate the events in Jesus' life chronologically. Like an editor of a newspaper they moved stories and events around in their books in order to give a special focus to their Gospels. The result is that the stories in the four Gospels are not narrated in the same order. One must, therefore, be very careful when pointing out the process of image streaming in Jesus' thinking. What may be found when looking at the corresponding story in another Gospel, is a different angle. While this knowledge cautions us when working with the Biblical text, very clear examples of image streaming in Jesus' thinking can be pointed out. Let us look at seven such examples:

The bread of life

(John 6)

We read in John 6 that Jesus used five loaves of bread and two fishes to feed a crowd. John the Evangelist tells in the following verses of this chapter how Jesus constructs a sermon around this event.

Jesus takes the physical bread, turns it into spiritual bread and calls Himself the bread of life. According to John, Jesus used the miracle of the bread and fish as an introduction to His talk on the bread of life. Although this conversation about Jesus being the bread of life is not found in the other Gospels, it is worthwhile looking at how John presents it to us.

The more Jesus focuses on the image of bread, the more details emerge. One can almost compare the concept of image streaming with a glass elevator moving from one floor to the other. You are standing inside the elevator looking out. The higher you go, the more detail you see. In verse 27 Jesus tells His disciples not to *"work for food that spoils, but for food that endures to eternal life, which the son of Man will give you."* In Jesus' mind it seems to conjure up the image of the manna the

Israelites ate in the desert. Now as the elevator goes higher, we see that this bread actually comes from God the Father. This God does not only give us bread, He also gives us life – in fact, eternal life.

Then Jesus elaborates on this image by saying He is the bread and that when we eat what He offers, we shall never go hungry again. Jesus expands the image further in verse 51 by telling His audience that His body is actually the bread He gives. He will give His body so that we may live. Now the glass elevator is just too high for His audience. They do not understand and start mumbling among themselves, wondering if Jesus is going to give His body for them to eat. But then Jesus takes them even further on this road of discovery, by saying that they will not only eat His body, they will also drink His blood. His body is the real food, His blood is real drink. Whoever eats this bread and drinks this blood will be given eternal life.

These images all came true when Jesus laid down His life so that humankind could be reconciled with God.

The good shepherd

(John 10)

In John 10 Jesus uses an image that was well known to the ancient sheep farmers. He also elaborates on it in great detail. He starts off by referring to a sheepfold. There are always thieves and robbers looking for personal gain. In order to reach their goal, they will climb over the walls of the fold. Jesus probably refers to the religious leaders who cared only about themselves.

Then Jesus elaborates further. There is a shepherd who does not come to the fold with evil intentions. He uses the gate. This is Jesus. The image expands: There is a relationship of trust between the shepherd and the sheep. They listen to his voice. The reverse is also true: The shepherd knows his sheep.

In the verses that follow Jesus gives more detail: The shepherd leads the sheep and they follow him. In the ancient world a shepherd never walked behind his sheep and drove them, but he walked ahead so that they could follow him. Jesus points out that sheep will never follow a shepherd they do not know.

As the glass elevator moves higher, we see a further stream of images Jesus creates in this conversation. He suddenly changes the image and says that He is the entrance (gate) to the fold (earlier on He was the shepherd). A sheep can only go into the fold through the entrance or gate. Likewise we can enter the Kingdom of God only through Jesus and through nobody else. Thieves kill the sheep. Jesus, in contrast, has only one objective and that is to let His sheep live.

The stream of images does not end here. A shepherd who does not love his sheep will run away when a wolf approaches. The wolf will have all the time in the world to devour the sheep. But Jesus cares for His sheep, because He is the good shepherd. He is even prepared to be killed as long as his sheep can live.

The images still continue. There is not only one flock. In Jesus' flock there are not only Jews. He will round up all the different flocks and they will all have only one shepherd – Jesus! In verses 19-21 we can see that the glass elevator has once again gone too high for His audience. They cannot grasp the meaning of Jesus' stream of images.

The true vine

(John 15)

This time Jesus uses a stream of images from the vineyard. One should take into account that this does not mean Jesus' images would be exclusively meaningful to only a certain group of people (the vineyard farmers). In ancient times almost every person had his own vineyard.

A farmer prunes the branches that bear fruit so that they can bear even more fruit. The opposite is also true, namely that he cuts off those branches that bear no fruit. With this image Jesus shows that people who are mere spectators of the Gospels and not really fruit-bearing followers, have no place in God's Kingdom.

More detail follows: No branch can bear fruit on its own. To be able to bear fruit, a branch must be attached to the vine – grow from it. Likewise no person can bear fruit if he or she is not connected to Christ. There is no way we can bear fruit on our own without God's cultivation. Branches that do not bear fruit are simply thrown away. Something happens to them: they dry out! Then Jesus takes the image a step further when He says that a farmer usually gathers these dry branches and puts them in the fire. This image is thus expanded to illustrate the condemnation of a person who does not bear fruit.

A little later Jesus elaborates further on this image by showing His followers that if they do bear fruit, they glorify God. What is more:

This is the very reason why God has called us.

It is indeed illuminating to see how Jesus' images stream one after the other. Like the bloom of a flower that opens up and reveals more beauty, Jesus' images unfold to illustrate more and more eternal truths.

About John the Baptist

(Matthew 11)

The images that are used need not all come from the same environment. For example, when Jesus talks about John, He initially uses an image of a reed in the wind (Matt 11:7). Jesus asks the people whom they think they will see in the desert when they go there: a reed being blown to and fro in the wind? But John is definitely not so inconsistent.

Subsequently Jesus uses the image of a man dressed in expensive clothes. But once again this is not John portrayed in the image. Then Jesus uses a new image: A number of children sit in the marketplace in two groups. One group plays a flute, but the other group will not dance. Then they play a mournful song, but the others do not react and will not cry. With these images Jesus illustrates His own ministry as well as John's. Nothing that Jesus or John does, satisfies the people. They are dissatisfied with everything because their warped expectations are not met. In this conversation regarding the ministry of Jesus and John, Jesus takes the images from a variety of other sources.

On the sorrows of life

(Luke 12:22-34)

When Jesus advises His followers to trust God because He will take care of them at all times, He uses different images. Firstly, He refers to the ravens that do not sow or reap, yet God provides for them. Then He conjures up the image of flowers that cannot make their own clothes, yet they are lovelier than Solomon in all his glory.

Then Jesus uses the image of grass. Very few people regard grass as very valuable. One day the grass is blooming, but the next day it withers and is thrown into the fire. If God makes this 'useless' grass so beautiful, surely He will take care of His people as well. Then Jesus uses the image of sheep when He addresses His followers as follows,

"Do not be afraid, little flock, for your Father has been pleased to give you the kingdom." (Luke 12:32)

By calling His listeners the 'little flock', Jesus shows wonderful compassion. It immediately recalls the image of the shepherd. In this way Jesus wants to assure His listeners that they have nothing to fear, because God the Father takes care of them like a shepherd.

A tree and its fruit

(Luke 6:43-45)

In these few verses we get a beautiful example of image streaming. Jesus provides more and more detail about the image He sees, and in this way His message has a powerful effect on the listener. Jesus teaches His disciples how important it is that one's actions should be in keeping with one's beliefs.

Jesus explains that a good tree cannot bear bad fruit. But then He changes the image around to say that a bad tree also does not produce good fruit. With this Jesus shows His disciples that one's lifestyle flows from the inner self. Then He paints a picture of a thorn bush that bears figs, and of one that bears grapes. This image is one of impossibility – nature just does not allow this to happen. In conclusion Jesus uses an idiom rich in visual connotations: *"Out of the overflow of your heart your mouth speaks."* As these images unfold, the full realisation emerges that we should balance our lives according to what we profess.

Dr Kobus Neethling | Prof Hennie Stander | Dr Raché Rutherford

The Parable of the Sower

(Matthew 13)

The well-known parable of the sower is actually quite remarkable because it is the only parable Jesus Himself explains in detail to His listeners. This is not simply a single image Jesus uses, but because He talks about it and provides more and more detail, He conveys a very powerful message.

Jesus starts by telling of the man who sowed seeds. Some fell on the footpath and the birds came and ate them. Some fell on rocky places where there was little soil. They came up quickly, but could not take root properly in the shallow soil. Thus, when the sun became hot, they wilted. Other seeds fell among the thorns, which choked them. The rest of the seeds landed on fertile soil and produced a good crop.

His disciples cannot understand the parable, therefore Jesus elaborates further on the parable of the sower to make it clear to them. He says the image of the seeds that fall on the footpath refers to the evil person who takes away the seeds that are sown in his/her heart. The man with whom the seeds fall on rocky places is he who hears the Word and immediately accepts it with joy. Unfortunately it does not take root and he soon becomes disloyal. The one where the seeds fall among the thorns is he who hears the Word, but the worries of life choke it. He also never bears fruit. But the man with whom the seeds fall on fertile soil is he who hears the Word and understands it. He, indeed, bears fruit and produces a good crop.

Undoubtedly Jesus is a wonderful example of someone who makes use of image streaming in a fascinating way.

- Paul Torrance, well-known writer and creativity expert, said as far back as 1959, *"In almost every field of human achievement, creativity is usually the distinguishing characteristic of the truly eminent."* More than ever creativity is an essential skill for people who want to achieve success in this age of rapid change. Creativity *"happens"* when in our thinking we make connections and keep our thinking open to what can flow from it and develop into new ideas. This is precisely what image streaming is – keeping the idea channels of the conscious and subconscious mind open in order to gain new insights.

- Often solutions elude us because we close our thinking; we anchor to one possibility only. Image streaming is the *"unlocking"* of this closed door; it is allowing other ideas to stream in even if they do not seem to make sense at the moment.

- People of the 21st century very seldom allow themselves moments of silent withdrawal, meditation and relaxation. It is, indeed, during these moments that we truly pick the positive fruits of image streaming. When we allow our thinking to produce images in a natural, unforced way, certain situations and problems become clear from the thinking and the images that flow from the subconscious. Try such an image streaming exercise by making use of a tape recorder. Think your problem or situation through, and as your thoughts (even if they sound far-fetched and totally disconnected) enter your mind, say them aloud. Play back the recording later, while you keep an open mind, and you will be amazed at the connections and insights you are capable of.

> " *What the inner voice says will not disappoint the hoping soul.* "

Dr Kobus Neethling | Prof Hennie Stander | Dr Raché Rutherford

SEVEN

SYSTEM THINKING –
WHEN THE BUTTERFLY FLAPS ITS WINGS IN MIAMI, IT HAILS IN BEIJING

In this chapter we want to:

- explain the concept of *"system thinking"* briefly
- endorse the importance of system thinking – a perspective of great importance to every human being
- point out examples which portray Jesus as an outstanding system thinker

The poet John Donne (1572 – 1631) explained poetic system thinking as follows: *"No man is an island entire of itself; every man is a part of the main. Any man's death diminishes me because I am involved in mankind and therefore never send to know for whom the bell tolls, it tolls for me."*

In 1990 Peter Senge, as a result of his book The Fifth Discipline, popularised the concept of system thinking internationally. However, there were many others before Senge who challenged, during the second half of the previous century, the old paradigm that attempted to divide human beings and their world into separate fragments. Fritjof Capra, famous system theorist, physicist and author of international best sellers like The Turning Point and Uncommon Wisdom, endorsed the *"interrelatedness"* of all the factors in the environment and the economy. In the seventies and eighties there were brilliant contributions to the system debate: Kenneth E Boulding's The World as a Total System (1985), C. Churchman's The Systems Approach and its Enemies and Ludwig van Bertalanffy's Perspectives: a General Systems Theory (1975).

System thinking is seeing further and deeper than the obvious isolation of things and noticing both the apparent as well as the hidden patterns. Then when we see these connections between factors, we are much more able to understand and influence the process. In short: a system is something that maintains its existence and functions through the interaction of its parts. The human body is a perfect example of a system. It consists of various parts and organs, each with its own functions. Each operates separately, yet they co-operate and influence one another. If no blood flows to the feet, you cannot walk; if your hand aches, it affects the whole body; if you develop a lung ailment it retards the movements of the entire body.

A school, an organisation, a team, family, congregation and a business (the list is endless) are all systems with their own unique shapes and interconnectedness.

- The poor service of the bank teller when he/she treats his/her clients badly, cannot be judged in isolation. To the clients this teller becomes the bank as a whole. His/her service affects the total image of the bank.
- Skin irritations that people develop in a certain area may be the direct result of polluted smoke from factories in the vicinity.
- A player in a team can, because of his/her persistently negative

attitude and lack of dedication, influence the performance of the whole team negatively.
- An unstable political situation in one country can exert pressure on the economy of adjacent countries.

It is a fact that human beings are systems in themselves and that they cannot have meaningful existences unless they understand and manage themselves as systems. The same insight into the social systems of our world is imperative and indispensable. What is of critical importance is to realise that if you remove parts of a system, you are not left with a few systems, but probably only one system that does not function well. If you take the receptionist away from the reception desk, you do not have two systems – you have only one that delivers poor service.

The advantages of system thinking are:

- Because you start seeing patterns, you will have better control over yourself, your health, your spiritual life, your relationships and your general circumstances.
- You will be able to find better solutions and handle problems within a wider context.
- You will work smarter, not necessarily harder, because you will be able to see the essence of circumstances in the big picture.
- You will be able to handle and predict the future more accurately because you can interpret the patterns of change and future development more clearly.
- You will be a much better manager of your thinking and emotions because you will not judge your emotions and those of other people around you on a minute to minute basis. You will

rather interpret behaviour within the bigger picture (blame, hate, anger will make room for understanding, compassion, empathy).
- You will be able to guide and mentor the group, the family, the team, the congregation and the business you find yourself in more meaningfully.

Once again we find the fundamental truths of system thinking in the Bible.

Examples from the Bible

Jesus was first and foremost someone who could see deeper and further than the obvious. Let us consider seven examples where He looked much further than the few isolated events before Him:

The crucifixion of Jesus

(Luke 23:26-43)

Jesus' conduct during His crucifixion is undoubtedly one of the best examples one can find of someone who is able to retain perspective at all times. Jesus sees a much wider picture and is not caught up in the events unfolding before Him and that are causing Him so much pain and suffering. He understands that it is all part of God's bigger plan with humankind. For this reason He is able to pray to God, even in His darkest hour, and ask, *"Father, forgive them, for they do not know what they are doing."* He also has compassion for His mother. When He sees her standing next to the disciple He loves, He says to her, *"Dear woman, here is your son,"* and to the disciple, *"Here is your mother."*

Because Jesus does not get caught up in what is so obvious in this event, He is able to see beyond the immediate moment.

The woman who had been bleeding for twelve years

(Mark 5:21-43)

We read in Mark 5 about a woman who continually menstruated for 12 years. It caused her great discomfort and doctors could do nothing for her. In fact, her condition slowly deteriorated. In the ancient world this problem would be much worse because a woman was considered 'unclean' during her menstruation period. This was why she went to Jesus filled with hope. Quite unobtrusively she touched His clothes, and was instantly cured. But Jesus noticed that healing power had gone out of Him and asked who had touched His clothing. The woman was alarmed and started shivering. She fell on her knees in front of Him and told Him her history. Then Jesus said to her, *"Daughter, your faith has healed you. Go in peace and be freed of your suffering."*

What makes this event so remarkable is that this woman only craved physical healing. That she received. But afterwards she would have experienced a tremendous feeling of guilt, because she knew the social norms of her time only too well. She would have known that when an 'unclean' woman touched a 'holy' rabbi, she made the rabbi 'unclean' as well. Her physical healing would have brought her a heavy burden of guilt. But Jesus did not leave it there. He let her tell everything in public. Consequently His words (*"Go in peace"*) must have given her a wonderful feeling of liberation. Never again would she need to feel guilty about her healing. Nobody would scorn her, because the rabbi Jesus had publicly sent her away in peace.

In this story we see how Jesus sees a much bigger picture than merely the physical problem of a woman. Jesus also understands how society deals with menstruating women and He grasps the extent of the guilt she has been burdened with. Because He looked much wider than the scene being enacted before Him, He could offer her total peace and comfort.

The entry into Jerusalem

(Luke 19:28-44; Matthew 21:1-11)

The crowd accompanied Jesus as He rode into Jerusalem on a donkey. While Jesus was riding they stripped off their coats and spread them on the road. They also broke branches from the trees and spread them on the road too. It was their way of honouring Him. The crowds cheered and praised God for all the miracles they had seen. It was clear that they worshipped Jesus as their Christ and King. The Pharisees were irritated and angered. They asked Jesus to silence His followers, but Jesus summed up the situation and said that if they kept quiet, the stones would shout it out.

In spite of this aggressive opposition Jesus does not act irrationally or with emotional immaturity. He sees much deeper and further.

That is why we read in verses 41-42 that when He approaches the city, He cries and says, *"If you...had only known on this day what would bring you peace – but now it is hidden from your eyes."* Jesus sees more than the events taking place before His eyes. He is sad because the people in the city do not realise what is happening. The peace they are singing about in verse 38 is indeed available in this city, but they do not realise it. Therefore Jesus knows that difficult times await Him.

It is also very clear, from these events, that Jesus is constantly acutely aware of the bigger picture and sees the connections which seem so invisible to others.

Jesus heals a paralysed man

(Matthew 9:1-8)

We read in Matthew 9 that people bring a paralysed man to Jesus. We expect to read that Jesus heals him immediately, but to our surprise we hear Jesus saying to him, *"Take heart, son; your sins are forgiven."* With this Jesus does not indicate any correlation between the man's illness and his sins. The point is that Jesus does not merely focus on the man's disease. He looks much deeper. He sees the man's greater need and wants to bring him salvation on a much larger scale. Jesus wants to bring a complete cure. When Jesus finally heals him, being cured from his paralysis becomes the proof of his total recovery.

Once again we notice that Jesus sees beyond the moment; beyond the immediate world.

The woman with the alabaster jar of perfume

(Luke 7:36-50)

When Jesus was invited to dine at the home of Simon the Pharisee, a sinful woman arrived there. She had an alabaster jar of perfume with her. She knelt behind Jesus' feet and wept. Later her tears fell on His feet and she dried them with her hair. Then she kissed His feet and anointed them with her perfume. Simon thought that if Jesus had been a prophet He would have known that she was a sinful woman. Then Jesus told Simon the parable to show him that the woman was sad because she realised the extent of her sinful life. Thereupon He forgave her sins.

Again Jesus does not see a weeping woman in front of him. He looks much deeper and realises why she is sad. Thus He can give her absolution. But Jesus also looks deeper into the heart of Simon. He knows what is on his mind and thus tells him the parable to put the matter into perspective. And this is what Jesus does every time; He puts the issue, the event or conflict into a far greater context – creating meaning and insight that have not been there before. He succeeds in recognising a bigger issue – something more than the small event unfolding in front of Him. This contributes to His bringing so much more deliverance to the people around Him.

The widow's tiny offering

(Luke 21)

While Jesus is in the temple He sees some rich people putting a lot of money into the temple collection box. Subsequently a poor widow comes and puts in only two small coins. Jesus sums up the situation at a glance. He sees far more than only a poor widow and two little coins. Her whole world of abject poverty and humility, but also the sincerity and dedication with which she brings her money, becomes clear to Him. In sharp contrast He sees right through the show and pomp of the rich. Then Jesus says, *"I tell you the truth… this poor widow has put in more than all the others. All these people gave their gifts out of their wealth, but she out of her poverty put in all she had to live on."*

Because Jesus sees more than the obvious, He judges a situation with so much more sensitivity and caring. He understands the essence of what is happening here, and is therefore able to exercise His influence to bring about dynamic change.

A great commission for the disciples

(Matthew 28:19-20)

Jesus was a Jew and His appearances were restricted to certain regions of Palestine. But He was well aware of the fact that His actions had dramatic impact much further afield. He realised that everything fitted into God's plans, and that His message was in effect meant for all humankind. That is why Jesus, after His resurrection, called all His disciples together and said to them, *"Therefore go and make disciples of all nations, baptizing them in the name of the Father and the Son and the Holy Spirit, and teaching them to obey everything I have commanded you. And surely I am with you always, to the very end of the age."*

Jesus' vision was much more encompassing than only for Palestine and what was happening there.

The above-mentioned examples and many others once again underline the fact that Jesus excelled at inter-connecting; seeing and realizing how every moment linked with another moment; not focusing on the detail but the position of the detail within the bigger framework of things – He saw bigger and further and was at all times able to connect and to synthesise.

System thinking for a changing world

The technological explosion has made the modern person realise full well that he/she is not on an island, but part and parcel of a wider society – part of a dynamic system. An apparently insignificant event in one part of the world may have a rippling effect and may even affect the economies of other countries. The better we understand this bigger context of our own lives and the environments we live in, the easier it will be to solve problems and find solutions.

- There are few people who do not realise that pollution, bad eating habits, no exercise, smoking, little sleep, etc., are detrimental to their health. It is the responsibility of the individual to make the right choices in order to limit these negative influences. We must realise, however, that these external, physical elements only form part of a larger system. Within this system a positive attitude, constructive relationships and future visions play an important part in the overall *"feeling good"* system. Therefore it does not help to make the right choices as far as concrete matters alone are concerned. Health has a much deeper meaning and forms part of a much wider context.
- In the same way, if we are sensitive to it, we shall be able to link our physically *"low"* times with our thinking. Negative thinking leads to negative talking, that creates a negative atmosphere, which in turn influences not only us but also others to turn negative. This leads to physical illnesses and a general feeling of *"not being well"*. The modern person should see his/her thinking as the centre of the wider system of *"feeling well"*, of the joy of life!
- We often carry with us heavy baggage from the past. It spoils our lives and our futures. It is now the time to empty these bags and put the things in their proper places within the systems of our lives – and to see how they pale into insignificance against the big picture. When people upset you, make you angry,

disappoint you, see these things for what they are – a moment in the bigger picture of your life, but definitely not your life! Give them the time and attention a moment deserves, but do not devote your life to them.

Dr Kobus Neethling | Prof Hennie Stander | Dr Raché Rutherford

EIGHT

"OUT OF THE BOX" THINKING – EVERY EXIT IS AN ENTRANCE TO SOMETHING ELSE

In this chapter we want to:

- explain what *"out of the box thinking"* means
- highlight the importance of *"out of the box thinking"* for a changing world
- illustrate *"out of the box thinking"* as Jesus' unique thinking preference

In the eighties of the previous century Joel Barker popularised the term *"paradigm"* and it became a popular buzz word of the eighties and nineties. But it was actually the historian Thomas S. Kuhn who 20 years previously developed a theory that addressed the process of paradigm shifting very specifically. He defined a paradigm as a belief system or set of rules that a person or organisation develops over time. The paradigm then creates the boundaries in which you function and operate; you begin to develop the skills and attitudes to perform within those boundaries and eventually you become very comfortable within those parameters.

Concepts generally associated with paradigms are:
- habit
- rule/regulation
- method
- doctrine
- law
- convention
- dogma
- tradition
- routine
- practice
- theory
- ideology
- ritual

The paradigm, whether it is the rule, tradition, paradigm concept, or whatever, sets the parameters within which you think and act – and then you develop behaviour patterns that enable you to function within these parameters. What often happens is that one becomes so used to the boundaries that one becomes blind to what happens beyond them.

This way of looking with half-closed eyes at the world is found in every aspect of life. It causes rigidity and a kind of denial of the realities of the time and space we find ourselves in. It is not only the ordinary person who develops paradigm blindness – church leaders, business leaders, scientists, political leaders, sports leaders, educationists; almost in every field one can think of there is a general inclination towards *"inside the box"* thinking. Within individual or organisational frameworks it happens that paradigms are transferred from generation to generation. I run my family along the same lines my father did; or I supervise my subordinates the way it has been done in this business for years; or I follow the methods of teaching the way they have been practised for ages. The list is endless.

Typical comments of the paradigm person or establishment are often:
- This is how it has always been done here

- You with your new, foolish ideas
- Wait till you have been here as long as we have, or till you know as much as we know, then you will change your tune
- Get real!
- It is against the rules, doctrine, policy, therefore it may not be done
- You are upsetting the order and the peace

It is ironical that throughout the ages it has always been the *"out of the box"* thinkers that changed the course of history, that made breakthroughs and have been responsible for the innovations and changes that have made our planet a better place. Surely it is not wrong to stick to certain rules and structures. They are often very useful and functional:
- the seven step-by-step things I do in the mornings before school or work prevent chaos in the household
- traffic rules prevent anarchy on the roads and are an internationally accepted paradigm
- every kind of sport is played according to certain rules and directives
- religion has dogma and order as its foundation

A list of paradigms can probably be compiled for every institution, but every paradigm eventually develops problems and causes conflict. If it is not addressed creatively, challenged and changed, the same rules that made yesterday so successful can be the destroyers of today. It has never been more important than now to analyse and to challenge consistently the effect and meaning of every custom, habit and rule. Precisely because of the tempo that will keep accelerating during this century, we shall literally and figuratively die if we do not become challengers and innovators of paradigms. The extraordinary changes of the past two decades indicate that the changes happening right now, are already changing again. In most cases it is risky to challenge the existing order (and it is apparently safer inside the box), for the opposition is usually fierce. It is often dangerous to be a pioneer challenger, because everyone who was comfortable with the old set of rules (including the leaders) is virtually forced back to point zero. (The secretary who has always performed excellently on her old typewriter is forced to point zero by the introduction of a computer.)

Hate, anger, disappointment, disapproval and opposition are the emotions and behaviour especially caused by new paradigms. To create new insights, orders and playing fields calls for exceptional wisdom, faith, creativity and perseverance. The inspirational leadership of the original *"out of the box"* thinker and the courage of his/her supporters who help to renew and change the thinking of the individual, the group, the society and the community, are the critical factors that create acceptance of the new movement, order, product or game.

The initial followers and supporters of the *"out of the box"* thinker usually experience the suspicion and enmity of the majority. Faith in the new way of thinking is essential – to believe that it is the correct path to follow; to believe that the old way of doing will eventually fail; to believe in perseverance despite fierce opposition.

Courage, intuition and the creative searching and finding of alternative ideas and solutions are essential characteristics of the *"out of the box"* thinker.

Examples from the Bible

Jesus was the perfect example of an *"out of the box"* thinker. In fact, He shocked the people of His time to such an extent with His *"new way of thinking"* that they eventually crucified Him.

Jesus told a beautiful parable to indicate how radically His teachings contrasted with the traditional beliefs of His time. In Luke 5: 37-38 Jesus says, *"And no one pours new wine into old wineskins. If he does, the new wine will burst the skins, the wine will run out and the wineskins will be ruined. No, new wine must be poured into new wineskins."*

In Biblical times wine was kept in containers made of goatskin. When the wineskins were new they were elastic enough to withstand the chemical reaction of the new wine. Should one, however, pour new wine into an old wineskin that had lost its elasticity, it could cause the container to burst and one would lose the wine.

Jesus uses this image to compare the Pharisees to the old wineskins. They were so rigid and caught up in their traditions and rules that they could not accommodate His new teachings. That is why they were so antagonistic towards Him. But what was so new about Jesus' teachings? Let us look at seven examples in which His teachings broke drastically with traditional beliefs:

The love commandment

(John 13:34)

In John 13:34 Jesus says, *"A new command I give to you: Love one another. As I have loved you, so you must love one another."*

We may argue that this love commandment is not so new. We do read in Leviticus 19:18, *"Do not seek revenge or bear a grudge against one of your people, but love your neighbour as yourself. I am the Lord."*

For this reason one theologian prefers to translate the verse as follows: *"I give you it anew."* In this way he wants to indicate that Jesus does not give a new commandment, He only renews it. However, the verse cannot be translated like this. But we do ask ourselves what it is that is indeed new about Jesus' commandment.

The newness lies in the motive for our love. We must love others *"as Christ loved us"*. Jesus shows us that love means that one should be willing to sacrifice oneself for one's neighbour. It is precisely what Jesus does when He, because of His love for humankind, is prepared to die on the cross. This kind of love is totally different to that which the Pharisees and teachers of the law taught the people.

From Matthew 5:43 we gather that the scribes even believed that one should indeed love one's neighbour, but that one *"should hate one's enemy"*. This addition (to hate your enemy) appears nowhere in the Old Testament, but is the way the scribes interpreted it and taught the people. It gives us a very clear idea of what the average Jew was thinking in Jesus' time. But as *"out of the box"* thinker par excellence, Jesus broke radically with this popular belief and made even greater demands on His followers.

Breaking down barriers

(Matthew 18:21-35)

The Jews in Jesus' time placed all kinds of barriers and parameters around their commandments. These commandments were subject to various qualifications and conditions. Should a situation arise which fell outside these conditions, the prescriptions of the commandment would no longer prevail. Jesus came to break down the barriers and parameters.

Ancient Jewish text, for example, points out that God forgives humankind twice or at most three times for the same sin. According to them God will not forgive a fourth time. From this it was deducted that we should also be prepared to forgive our neighbour only three times. This traditional belief underlies Peter's question in Matthew 18:21, *"Lord, how many times shall I forgive my brother when he sins against me? Up to seven times?"*

Peter thinks that he is being very generous. He offers the possibility that one should forgive one's neighbour as often as seven times. But Jesus replies, *"I tell you, not seven times, but seventy times seven."* We must not interpret Jesus' answer literally as if He says we should forgive 490 times. On the contrary, His answer should be interpreted symbolically. Both the numbers 7 and 10 are the symbols of perfection. Jesus multiplies 7 with 10 and again with seven to indicate that there may be no boundary or limit to one's forgiveness. Thereby Jesus draws a line through this traditional belief.

It was typical of the Jews in the New Testament to indicate a point up to where a law was valid, and from where it was no longer valid. For example, we read in Luke 10:25 that Jesus reminds an expert on the law of these words, *"Love the Lord your God with all your heart and with all your soul and with all your strength and with all your mind, and love your neighbour as yourself."* Then we read, *"But he (the law expert) wanted to justify himself, so he asked Jesus, 'And who is my neighbour?'"*

What the question insinuates is that there are people who are not my neighbour. If a speaker should ask the people in his/her audience who does not live in New York, one can infer he assumes there are people who live elsewhere. Likewise we can infer from the learned man's question that he assumes that there are people who are not his/her neighbour. But Jesus breaks down these barriers and tells the story of the Good Samaritan. In this way Jesus teaches the teacher of religious law that even Jews and Samaritans should treat one another like neighbours.

To us in modern times it may not sound like a very new message, but to the Jews in Biblical times it was a very radical one.

With this doctrine Jesus directly opposes the current beliefs of His time. The Jews and Samaritans were arch-enemies. We read in John 4:9 that they did not want to have anything to do with one another. But Jesus brings His people a message that differs completely from what they are accustomed to.

Food laws

(Mark 7:14-21)

The Jews had strict laws about what they might eat and what not.

These laws were based on the Old Testament, and the teachers of these laws thrashed out their implications into fine detail. Because it concerned food, it meant that every Jew's life was controlled by these laws every day. It was a tremendous burden on the shoulders of every devout Jew.

In Mark 7:14-23 Jesus does away with these laws. He is very sharp in His remarks about the food laws. He says food cannot make one unclean. When one eats, the food goes to one's stomach and then leaves the body again when it is excreted. Jesus then warns His listeners to worry less about the food they eat and more about what comes from their hearts. Here one thinks of dirty thoughts, fraud, pride, adultery, avarice, and so forth.

In modern times we find it difficult to understand how radically Jesus' teachings about food differed from what the average Jew believed. A Jew who accepted Jesus' teachings and brought his life into line with them, would find out that his entire way of living had changed drastically. Jesus was the thinking pioneer, the challenger of outdated norms and beliefs and His *"out of the box"* nature caused tension amongst many of the people of His time.

Washing hands

(Matthew 15:1-5)

The Jews had strict laws which stipulated that they always had to wash their hands before a meal. This was, however, not for hygienic purposes. In fact, they did not wash their hands the way we imagine someone would wash his/her hands in a basin. The hand washing referred to here happened when someone (usually a servant) symbolically sprinkled a little water over your hands before you touched the food. It was merely a ritual that indicated you were now *"pure"* and could touch and eat *"pure"* food.

Jesus and His disciples, however, did not take these laws to heart. Thus we read in Matthew 15:1-2, *"Then some Pharisees and teachers of the law came to Jesus from Jerusalem and asked, 'Why do your disciples break the tradition of the elders? They don't wash their hands before they eat.'"*

In this passage Jesus points out to the Pharisees and the scribes that it is not the outward actions, like the washing of hands, that make a person sincere in his/her devotion to God. It is the attitude of the heart that matters. Again it is difficult for a modern person to imagine how agitated the Biblical Jews must have been when they saw that Jesus and His disciples did not wash their hands before eating.

Fasting and Praying

(Matthew 6:5-18)

In Biblical times people had all kinds of customs regarding praying and fasting. Many of them wanted other people to see and to know when they prayed and fasted. With such public piousness you could impress people and enhance your reputation. Therefore such hypocrites would even stand and pray in the streets. As a matter of fact, they often stood on the street corners where people could see them from all sides. When they fasted, they did not wash their faces, they put ashes on their heads and went about with long faces so that everyone who encountered them would know they were fasting.

Jesus breaks these customs. In Matthew 6:5-18 He teaches the people that they should rather go into their rooms and pray to God in private. He cautions them to take care of their appearance so that others cannot see that they are fasting. Their heavenly Father does not need the outward charade to know that they are fasting.

Jesus' teachings are once again in direct contrast to the customs of the time. To the devout it must have been a revolutionary change in religious practice.

The Sabbath

(Mark 2:23-28)

The Sabbath was very important to the Jews in New Testament times. They thrashed out the Old Testament laws concerning the Sabbath into great detail. One of the Ten Commandments reads as follows, *"For in six days the Lord made the heavens and the earth, the sea, and all that is in them, but he rested on the seventh day. Therefore the Lord blessed the Sabbath day and made it holy."* (Exodus 20:11)

But the scribes worked out in detail how to apply this law in daily life. They taught the people that they were not even allowed to pull a gray hair from their heads on the Sabbath. Should they do it, they would be *"harvesting"* and because harvesting was work, they would desecrate the Sabbath.

In Mark 2:23-24 we read, *"One Sabbath Jesus was going through the grainfields, and as his disciples walked along, they began to pick some heads of grain. The Pharisees said to him, 'Look, why are they doing what is unlawful on the Sabbath?'"*

From the rest of the story it becomes clear how radically Jesus' views differ from those of the Pharisees. Jesus points out to them that God did not institute the Sabbath to make it difficult for His people, but rather to support them. In this way Jesus emphasises the freedom of the believer. This teaching of Jesus was also a drastic violation of a doctrine that ruled the lives of the ancient Jews.

Communicating with women in public

(John 4:1-42)

Jesus not only broke dramatically with traditional beliefs in His teachings, He also did so in His way of life and His public appearances.

For instance, it was unthinkable that any man would have a conversation with a strange woman in public. Jesus did not hesitate to break this social taboo. In John 4 we read how He conversed with a woman who came to draw water from a well. To top it all, she was a Samaritan. We read in verse 27 that His disciples were astonished to see what He was doing. Because Jesus ignored this social habit of the Jews, He eventually won this woman for God's cause.

Jesus did not remain within the confines of the *"little boxes"* that characterised Jewish life at the time. He was an *"out of the box"* thinker, a paradigm shifter. He did not hesitate to draw a line through traditions and customs which were the order of the day.

Jesus' behaviour was innovative and He led His followers along the road of innovative thinking. And in the words of Paul Torrance *"Jesus as the creative genius was performing miracles although he was always on the verge of crucifixion."*

Jesus was an example par excellence of the *"out of the box"* thinker of His time. He shifted existing boundaries; challenged assumptions and traditional thinking; said and did things differently. That made Him different, unique and unacceptable to many people. People of the 21st century no longer have the luxury of a choice whether to be *"out of the box"* thinkers or not. In fact, in this era of rapid change, of entrepreneurship, of challenges and opportunities, it will only be the *"out of the box"* thinker that will survive in the true sense of the word.

- Leaders in all fields (the business world, politics, education) who do not have the courage to challenge rigid systems, will go under with these systems. When a leader clings to those systems because *"they have worked up to now"*, and he/she does not measure them up to present day needs and norms, the writing is on the wall.
- Parents who educate the way they were educated will have to reconsider. Of course we can learn many lessons from the way we were educated by our parents. However, the parents of today have to realise that the world in which their children live, and the world for which they have to prepare them, are completely different from the one their parents lived in. The challenge of the modern world is all about mentoring the child towards becoming a creatively and emotionally mature person. We have to fully understand the new life before we can complete this task successfully. Parents will have to make sure of the inner qualities of strength their children have to acquire

in order to journey through this world comfortably.
- In all fields of management (at home, the work place, the sports team, etc.) a big shift has taken place in the new century. Those who still cling to an authoritarian attitude of the 'boss' versus the subordinate who has to carry out commands, live in a different dimension of time. The environment that has been established over the last few decades creates is fertile soil for self-development, for innovative thinking at all levels, and for openness to the opinions and ideas of others.
- Those who smugly live and work in a comfort zone, who resist change and growth, will not only lag behind, they will die. The time for adapting and making small changes has passed. Our paradigm shifts must be big enough so that we can change creatively, revolutionary – even though we encounter resistance from those who desperately cling to a time that has already become an illusion.

> *In the 21st century an ark won't do, build surfboards.*
>
> **– W Grulke**

Dr Kobus Neethling | Prof Hennie Stander | Dr Raché Rutherford

NINE

WHOLE BRAIN THINKING –
TO LOOK WITH A FRESH PAIR OF EYES

In this chapter we want to:

- explain the whole brain concept
- emphasise the importance of whole brain thinking in our lives
- introduce Jesus as the ultimate whole brain thinker

For people with a keen sense of perception it has always been clear that every person has specific preferences for thinking and doing. Although the science of left and right brain thinking, as well as whole brain functioning, is fairly new, observations of individual behaviour and thinking preferences have been recorded for centuries. These dominant thinking preferences develop as a result of the individual's interaction with his/her family, his/her church, his/her school, his/her work, sport and social environments.

Thus the approaches one favours in problem solving, coping with different situations, decision making and effecting change are indicative of the unique thinking preferences each one of us has developed over time. For instance, one person will prefer to do in-depth research before he/she tackles a problem; another will plan first; another one will immediately discuss the matter with friends or colleagues and still another one will look at alternative options first.

The Nobel Prize winner Roger Sperry and his colleagues performed the first split brain operation where the communication channel between the left and the right brain, the corpus callosum, was separated. The two parts of the brain consequently functioned independently and for the first time it became scientifically possible to determine which functions were performed by the left and which functions were performed by the right brain.

Hermann's research in the seventies led to the four-quadrant model to explain brain preferences from four different perspectives. Although the four-quadrant theory had already existed for a long time, Hermann undoubtedly made a significant contribution.

In the eighties Kobus Neethling, under the mentorship of Paul Torrance from the University of Georgia, expanded the four-quadrant approach to a series of instruments and models to determine the brain profiles of children and adults. Apart from these instruments and models for general use, models were also developed for specific kinds of sports, parenting, coaching and relationships. Every person's specific thinking preferences indicate how he/she chooses to manage himself and other people, deal with problems, approach the future, teach and mentor people, make decisions, cope with challenges and conflict – indeed they give direction to every aspect of your life.

The challenge for every individual is to be comfortable with his or her own preferences, but surely also to observe the preferences of others correctly and effectively. When you have taken the first step to understand your own preferences and those of others, the second important step is to develop whole brain thinking skills in order to enable you to be an optimum achiever.

The concise exposition of the Whole Brain Model which follows here lays no claim to completeness. The objective is to make the reader aware of the primary thinking preferences associated with each of the quadrants, and then to illustrate Jesus' dominant thinking preferences as the point of departure for His behaviour as discussed in the preceding chapters.

What strikes us as remarkable is that Jesus constantly applied His whole brain to achieve His aim with people and circumstances. This means that as soon as He had applied His initial thinking preference to get the big picture of the situation, He used all the other quadrants to find the perfect solution. We believe there is a powerful message for all of us, namely that every one of us has a whole brain to be used – and that perhaps we cling too desperately to our dominant preferences.

Jesus sets the example – as the whole brain thinker He becomes the breakthrough leader; the innovator and meaningful change agent of His time and our time.

R1-Thinking preference:

- images (parables)
- systems
- big picture
- challenge

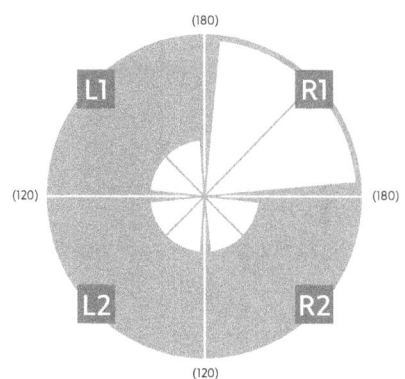

L1-Thinking preference:

- correct
- analytical
- focused
- factual

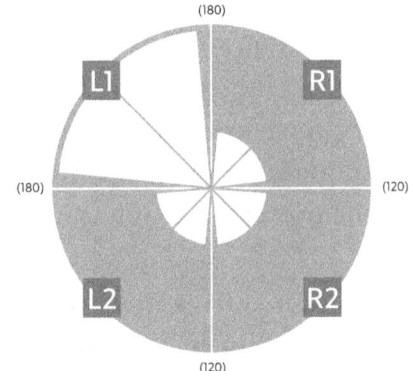

L2-Thinking preference:

- respect for order
- respect for specific institutions
- planning and thoroughness

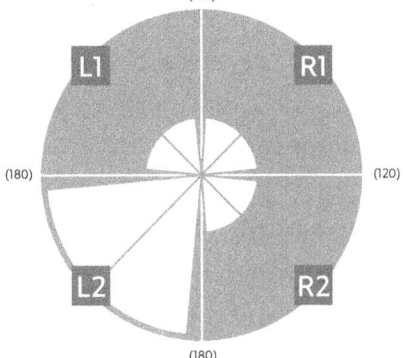

R2-Thinking preference:

- passion for fellow-humans
- empathy for others
- compassion for all (also the outsider)
- sensitivity

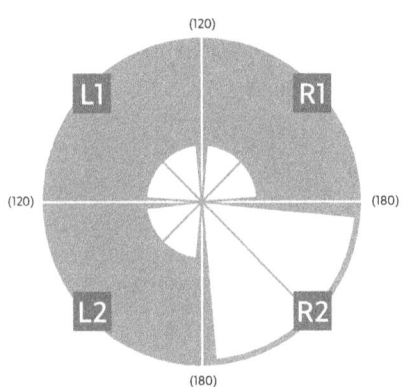

Although there are many examples where Jesus first took up a focused, analytical position (L1), or a traditional, structured approach (L2), or reacted with compassion and empathy (R2), His dominant preference was R1. Let us look at examples where Jesus used each of the quadrants as His point of departure.

R1   When Jesus wanted to emphasise to His disciples to what extent God was prepared to answer their prayers, He painted a very broad and visual picture of how they were always ready to help one another in times of need. When one of their friends knocked on their door and asked for a few loaves of bread for an unexpected guest, they would give immediately (Luke 11:5-8). How much more will God not be prepared to answer our prayers.

L1   When the scribes and the chief priests sent secret agents to corner Jesus, they confronted Him with the question whether it was right to pay taxes to Caesar (Luke 20:20-26). Jesus analysed their question logically and rationally, carefully considered the consequences of the various possible answers and gave a superb reply. The moment required a focused, logical response – and this is exactly what Jesus did.

L2   When Jesus' disciples asked Him to teach them to pray, He taught them an orderly, step-by-step prayer – The Lord's Prayer. (Luke 11:1-4)

R2   We read in John 11:33-35 *"When Jesus saw her (Mary) weeping, and the Jews who had come along with her also weeping, he was deeply moved in spirit and troubled. 'Where have you laid him (Lazarus)?' he asked. 'Come and see, Lord,' they replied. Jesus wept."* This story shows us with how much empathy Jesus reacted to His fellow human beings.

Jesus' dominant thinking preference and point of departure is the R1 quadrant. But there is no evidence that He valued it more than the other quadrants. It is precisely the continual use of the other quadrants that underlines the fact that He was a whole brain thinker. It is as if He tells us that we must first look at the big picture of ourselves and our relationship with God and our fellow human beings before we can begin to understand the big jig-saw puzzle of life and death. But the new idea, the moment of illumination and the breakthrough insight will soon fade without a process that leads to further knowledge, thorough planning and reaching out to others – and that is why Jesus points out to us the whole brain way.

Let us now look at some brilliant examples of His use of the whole brain thinking method:

Jesus clears the temple

(Luke 19:28-44)

When Jesus notices how people trade in the courtyard of the temple, He immediately sees the big picture (R1). He instantly grasps that the merchants are exploiting those who have come to worship. Because of His passion for the poor and the oppressed believers (R2), and because of His deep regard for the temple (L2), His actions are totally focused (L1) and systematic (L2) when He makes a whip and chases the merchants out.

This remains one of the most remarkable examples of whole brain thinking and it has retained its freshness to this day.

Jesus' entry into Jerusalem

(Luke 19:28-44)

Jesus enters Jerusalem on a donkey. He instantly grasps what is happening (R1) and understands the excitement of the crowd when they honour Him as the Christ. Because He analyses the situation correctly (L1) He knows there is no way of curbing the people's enthusiasm. Thus, when the Pharisees ask Him to silence His followers, He replies, *"I tell you …if they keep quiet, the stones will cry out."* However, when He sees Jerusalem in the distance and understands that the people will not accept the peace that can be theirs (R1 – the big picture), He becomes so sad that He weeps for them (R2). In great detail and step by step (L2) He explains to the people around Him what Jerusalem's future will be as a result of their stubbornness.

Jesus raises Lazarus

(John 11)

When Jesus hears that Lazarus is ill, He immediately sees the big picture, namely that Lazarus's illness will result in the revelation of God's miraculous power. The Son of God will eventually be glorified by this event (R1). When Lazarus dies and Jesus sees Mary weeping, He is deeply moved (R2). However, His reaction is completely rational (L1) and He asks to be taken to the grave. Step by step and fully conscious of all the conventions involved when a corpse has already been buried, He explains to the bystanders what to do (L2). After He has prayed and Lazarus has come out of the grave, Jesus tells them to remove the grave clothes.

In every situation, no matter how critical, Jesus uses all four the brain quadrants. That is why He succeeds in dealing with even the most unpleasant situation superbly.

The rich young man

(Mark 10:17-31)

A young man comes running to Jesus and says, *"Good Teacher… what must I do to inherit eternal life?"* Jesus looks much further than the immediate moment (R1) and says, *"No one is good – except God alone."* Very comprehensively and in a structured manner (L2) Jesus spells out the commandments to him. But when the young man replies that he has obeyed all the commandments since childhood, Jesus analyses the situation rationally and accurately (L1). He looks at the young man affectionately (R2) and says, *"One thing you lack… Go, sell everything you have and give it to the poor, and you will have treasure in heaven. Then come, follow me."*

Once again every brain quadrant is utilised in handling the young man's problem.

The request of James and John

(Mark 10:35-45)

James and John approach Jesus with a request: *"Teacher…we want you to do us a favour. In your glorious Kingdom, we want to sit in places of honour next to you…one at your right and the other at your left."* (NLT)
    It is obvious that these two disciples want to share in the glory of Jesus, but He sees something bigger (R1), namely that He is not about to be glorified, but rather to suffer and to die. Rationally (L1)

and systematically (L2) Jesus explains to them that there is no way for them to share what is awaiting Him. When the other disciples are indignant about the request, Jesus understands their emotions (R2). He reaches out to them and says that they should rather be prepared to serve than be served.

Jesus raises a widow's son at Nain

(Luke 7:11-17)

One day Jesus and His disciples go to a town called Nain. When they arrive there, they see a group of people carrying out a corpse to be buried. Jesus sees the big picture (R1): the dead person is the only son of a widow. The scene fills him with compassion (R2) and we read, *"When the Lord saw her his heart went out to her and he said, 'Don't cry.'"* He analyses the situation rationally (L1), then He approaches and touches the coffin. In a controlled, systematic manner (L2) Jesus waits for the bearers to stop, then He raises the child and gives him back to his mother.

Because Jesus once again applies His whole brain, He succeeds in transforming, carefully and compassionately, a very sad moment into one that leads to the glorification of God.

Jesus feeds five thousand people

(Mark:6:35)

Jesus' disciples point out to Him that they are at a remote place and it is getting late. They ask Him, therefore, to send away the people so that they can buy themselves some food. But Jesus sees much further than the narrow confines of the situation (R1). Because He feels sorry for the people (R2) He orders His disciples to provide food for the crowd. Very realistically He analyses the situation (L1) and asks how many loaves of bread they have. Then He acts in an organised manner as He orders the people to sit on the grass in small groups so that they can eat (L2). Then He multiplies the food His disciples have brought Him (five loaves of bread and two small fish) and distributes it among the people.

Once again He calmly and rationally solves a problem – because He sees beyond the moment and beyond the parameters of the immediate world.

When one looks at these examples from a whole brain perspective, they become new and almost breathtakingly relevant to the current world. Jesus sets an exceptional example of a whole brain in action an example which was so often not acknowledged or experienced in the past as a result of narrow-mindedness and short-sightedness.

People of this century have already started to experiment with concepts like individualism, uniqueness, non-conformity and diversity. The concept of whole brain thinking encompasses all of them. However, the scope and application possibilities of this concept in the present century are overwhelmingly impressive. There is simply no environment or situation where the application of whole brain thinking does not hold limitless advantages.

- The preacher who realises that his congregation consists of people with different preferences will prepare his sermons so that he can reach everyone (whether they prefer facts, analysis, structure, emotions or the big picture).
- Businesses where people are appointed to positions where their brain preferences and job descriptions coincide, will not only have employees who have the necessary skills, but also

staff members who enjoy their work and therefore have the passion and energy to be very productive.
- Any group, establishment, committee, etc., that deliberately composes its groups so that they consist of members whose preferences differ (thus a whole brain group), will be amazed at the solutions, decisions and arrangements that are right on target. Such a group puts all the important elements on the table (the financial implications, the essential procedures, staff issues, and the big picture) so that nothing of importance is overlooked.
- The parent who forces his/her own preferences onto his/her child, or who has no understanding of a child whose brain preferences differ drastically from those of the rest of the family, breaks down delicate relationships. The parent must realise that his/her child often thinks differently, but that does not mean he/she is necessarily wrong.
- Education can only be effective when it is based on whole brain principles. Teachers whose style has become bogged down in their own preferences, who never teach, set papers, give projects that accommodate the brain preferences of all the students, are not 21st century teachers.
- Whole brain thinking and its application means reaching out to others even if their thinking differs radically from mine. It teaches us tolerance and understanding of other people, as well as appreciating those who think differently. They fill that part of the whole brain that I cannot.

> *We must dare to think the unthinkable thoughts.*
>
> **– JW Fullbright**

Dr Kobus Neethling | Prof Hennie Stander | Dr Raché Rutherford

TEN

JESUS' MODEL FOR THE 21ST CENTURY

Self-help books are certainly not in short supply these days. Writers offer advice on improving relationships, how to run successful businesses, how to cope with fears, anger, depression, etc. The topics are legion, the opinions diverse, and the problems we have to face nowadays apparently infinite. In the process of writing this book it became increasingly clear: Jesus, through His extraordinary thinking, creatively solved every complex situation He was confronted with.

Jesus is the ultimate example of an extraordinary thinker confronted with much resistance, rejection, conflict, challenges, problems, group pressure, suffering, death. In the different chapters of this book, we studied and analysed His thinking processes in different and diverse circumstances and made them applicable to people of today. In conclusion, let us look at Jesus' extraordinary model for the 21st century – a thinking and doing model uniquely relevant for our times.

The Jesus-model for relationships

- Jesus deals with people in different ways. He accepts their differences and the fact that people have various needs (e.g. the visit to Martha and Mary).
- Jesus acts intuitively (whether it is godly foreknowledge or human intuition, it is an important part of His behaviour towards people). He reads the state of mind as well as the needs of people, and is therefore able to choose the correct words in every particular situation.
- Jesus accepts the validity of the emotions of the people around Him and does not hesitate to show His own. He weeps over Lazarus, He declares His love for His disciples and He admits His terrible fear in Gethsemane. Emotional intelligence and maturity are crucial ingredients in any relationship.
- His emotional maturity lets Him forgive (even the betrayer, the one who denies Him, and those who nail Him to the cross).
- Relationships often crumble because of monotony and a comfort zone developing between people. Jesus teaches us that we should always think innovatively and act with an element of surprise.
- We often do damage to relationships because we think, act and talk without thinking first. Jesus teaches us to think carefully about our actions in different situations and to realise that all kinds of conduct have specific outcomes.
- Jesus is sensitive, compassionate and empathic – the qualities that form the basis of successful relationships.

The Jesus-model for parenting

"Your hearts and minds must be made completely new." (Ephesians 4:23)
- Children are of utmost importance to Jesus: He even says the Kingdom of God is only meant for those who accept it like children. The example to parents is that Jesus not only shows love, but also understanding and respect for children.
- Even in stressful and upsetting situations, Jesus shows that nothing is achieved with anger. The lessons about life cannot be taught when discipline is based on strict control and fear.
- Jesus never expects a *"robot-reaction."* He listens to questions, arguments and opposition, and then reacts wisely.
- Parents who claim that they treat all their children equally are correct when it comes to money and material things. But Jesus is a striking example of how one should treat people differently with regard to their preferences and needs. Our children are unique beings and automatic, conditioned responses are unacceptable.
- Jesus says the eye is the lamp for the body and when the eye is good, your whole body has light, but when your eye is bad, not only is it without light but also your whole body is in darkness. This is how a parent's inputs fit into the bigger picture of his/her child's life: now and in the future.
- The world for which parents prepare their children differs drastically from that of their own youth. Like Jesus' thinking, parents' thinking should be open enough to accept renewal and change.
- Jesus filled His listeners with passion and interest: they were fascinated by His words and came from far and wide to listen to Him. How much passion and enthusiasm do we inspire in

our children or do they find us boring, passionless and without energy?

The Jesus-model for education

"Teach and instruct each other with all wisdom." (Colossians 3:16)
- Jesus was the most extraordinary teacher of all times. One of the most important elements of His life and conduct on earth was teaching people. Teachers often experience their important task as a process of *"suffering"* and they become negative about it. They should rather measure it against the great Teacher of all times and derive inspiration from Him.
- Jesus' teaching style was never authoritarian and His approach was never: *"I am the boss, I give orders, I am in control."* He rather introduced His listeners to new values through stories, metaphors and letting them see the big picture.
- Jesus' answer to many questions was a story. (The Good Samaritan, The Sower, the Mustard Seed, etc.) In this way His lessons became dynamic – part of the people's life experience and frame of reference. Instead of dry facts, these stories fitted like pieces of a puzzle into the broad pictures of their lives.
- Jesus did not tell people what to do – He was a mentor and facilitator who guided them to discover the values of life for themselves. In the 21st century we need mentors, not instructors.
- Jesus was above all the teacher who was 'different', who taught new truths. He was an *"out of the box thinker"* who made the world of His listeners new. In her book, Jesus in Blue Jeans, Laurie Beth Jones tells how she saw Jesus in a dream coming towards her in blue jeans. When He saw her surprise He asked

her why she was amazed. He said He had come to the world in a robe because the people wore robes, but He came to her in blue jeans because she wore blue jeans. The teacher of today needs blue jeans for the generation of today.
- Jesus was a courageous teacher. He taught many women (unheard of in His day!). He teaches them that it is not what goes into the mouth that makes people impure, it is what comes out of it, and He brings new insights about the Sabbath – shocking lessons at the time! The teacher who wants to prepare children adequately for this dynamic age, will have to be courageous.
- Like Jesus, teachers will have to be whole brain thinkers. They must not only understand themselves and their thinking preferences, but also that their classes consist of pupils who differ, who have various needs and behave differently in similar situations.

Jesus' model for the business world

- Jesus' model is clear: the successful business needs to take a fresh look at the world and existing paradigms must be questioned and tested to see if they will still *"work"* in this century.
- Business leaders will have to take the lead with new visions and will have to show courage in order to change as the environments of their businesses change. They must also expect to pay the price of unpopularity because of their new ideas, just like Jesus experienced the hostility of the Pharisees.
- Today's business will also have to act intuitively at times and not always revert to the exact, logical guidelines typical of businesses of the past. Is there still room for such thinking in this age? Of course, but the role of intuition, the *"gut feel"* about

what will work and what will not, will have to start taking over more and more.
- Businesses will have to understand and address the needs of their employees and customers. Like Jesus did, businesses must realise that every person is unique and in order to render the best possible service they have to probe this uniqueness creatively and innovatively.
- Businesses today need to see the big picture and understand their place and role in the bigger context.
- In the rat race of the 20th century, business leaders allowed themselves few breaks. What now when things are moving still faster and faster? It is essential to take a regular break so that we can give our thinking free rein, so that we can make connections which will eventually lead to new solutions.
- Top businessman and once the wealthiest person in the world, Bill Gates, said a few years ago. *"I don't play on someone else's playing fields, I create my own."* This is an example of *"out of the box"* thinking, one indication of meteoric success. Jesus teaches us that we have to jump out of our boxes so that we can discover and create the new playing fields of our age. He kept on challenging the old paradigms and creating new guidelines.

The Jesus-model for sport

- Nowadays there is not much distinction between the fitness and technological skills of top individuals or sports teams. It becomes increasingly clear that the critical factor that will make one team gain the victory over another, is their thinking. Like Jesus thinks deeply about every situation before He acts, it is of utmost importance for the successful sports team or person to

think likewise.
- We read in Peter 1:13: *"Gird up the loins of your mind."* (NKJV) *"So think clearly."* (NLT) *"Prepare your minds for action."* (NIV) The implication of this is that sportsmen must have a positive attitude, passion for the game and openness towards new ideas and insights.
- Jesus is a supreme example of a picture-thinker. The sports person or team that can visualise the victory prior to the match will develop coaching patterns to get the body ready at a much higher level than previously believed.
- Intuition plays an increasingly important role. This *"knowing without knowing"* is often more vital than the speed or fitness of a competitor.
- Sports teams and coaches who understand the thinking preferences of their players and approach team positions from this perspective, will have an incredible advantage. E.g. the soccer coach must have the insight that a person with a preference for spatial perception, variation and flexibility will make a good attacker. The more stable, orderly thinker will probably fit better into the defensive mode. Sport today also demands the whole brain approach.
- The sports team or person who wants to reach the top today must think creatively and innovatively. The downfall of many a team lies in its predictability and monotonous repetition. Playing not to lose – instead of playing to win.
- The successful sportsman will see the *"opening"* or gap, react to it with courage and flexibility, even if it was not exercised during the training programme.

The Jesus-model for problem solving

> "*... but let God transform you inwardly by a complete change of your mind.*"
>
> **– Romans 12:2**

- Jesus is constantly confronted with problems and difficult issues. It is clear that He never tries to evade the problems, but rather creates a climate conducive to finding solutions.
- Some of the issues He is confronted with are sensitive (Who is the most important in the Kingdom? What must I do to be saved? What must we pay Caesar? How can we feed the crowd on five loaves of bread and two fish?). Time and again His first reaction is to focus on solutions and not on problems. (He asks for a coin to solve the issue of taxes. He divides the crowd into small groups.)
- Jesus thinks differently and creatively about problems. He is impressed with the friends of the paralysed man who lower him through the roof. Creativity does not always mean major breakthroughs – it often means challenging the small and insignificant and making the little changes.
- Problem solving is not always a formal process. Jesus sees the gaps and uses situations and incidents to lead people to new insights.
- The answers to problems are often not where we are looking for them. Jesus teaches His listeners to jump out of their boxes and to look for answers outside the parameters of the known world. When the disciples were looking for guidelines to make their faith even stronger Jesus sketches the life of a slave: one who gives all without receiving anything in return. They receive a solution they did not expect.

- Jesus teaches us an important lesson when He solves problems: He first sees the essence of the problem. The rich young man's problem is not his good actions, it is his love for possessions.
- Jesus is also flexible when He is confronted with problems and realises that what applies to one person or situation does not apply to another. His conversation on divorce is a fine example of this. When His disciples conclude that it is better not to get married, He says, *"What you are saying now, is not possible for everybody."*

The Jesus-model for future visions

"What no man ever saw or heard, what no man ever thought could happen, is the very thing God prepared for those who love him."
– 1 Corinthians 2:9

- In the previous century it was still possible to create a future vision for the next 30 years and to pursue it systematically. The world today is too dynamic. When Jesus came to earth He upset His followers' plans for the future. We should see our future as flexible.
- The men who would eventually be known as His disciples had their futures mapped out. They were fishermen – they were born fishermen and expected to remain that for the rest of their lives. But Jesus inspires them to make a major paradigm shift – they leave their boats and nets and become *"fishers of people."*
- The current projection is that the school children of today will change jobs 20 times in their lifetime. The future is dynamic and the old concept of stability associated with the external environment (work, money, physical environment), must now

become an internal quality (intuition, creativity, openness, courage, passion, faith, dedication, etc.)
- The future makes many people nervous as a result of all the drastic changes, technology, and new insights. Jesus teaches us that we should use the apparent contradictions (paradoxes) of our time to our advantage, Thus we can experience truths more profoundly and gain new insights (e.g. to reach the top of the ladder is not necessarily success; the ladder must lean against the right wall. Our future vision determines how we experience it today. Destinations are merely starting blocks.)
- If we can become picture-thinkers like Jesus, people able to visualise our future, see the 'picture' of where we are going and feel it, our chances of actually realising it are so much more.

When His disciples want to know why Jesus talks in parables, thus why He always uses pictures, sees the big picture, and explains truths metaphorically, His answer is taken from Isaiah, *"You will hear my words but you will not understand; you will look but not see. The hearts of these people are hardened, their ears cannot hear and they have closed their eyes."*

If we do not start thinking like Jesus in a changing world, try to understand His way of thinking, and attempt to follow His example of extraordinary thinking, the above-mentioned accusation will be brought against us too.

THE FUTURE IS HERE

Some years ago, a concept like Artificial Intelligence, seemed farfetched. Today we live with it, and make use of it, often not even knowing that we are part of this growing phenomenon. We do E-payments, talk to Chatbots, switch on our autocorrect, and don't think twice about using facial recognition.

How do we align *"thinking like Jesus"* with a modern and often mind-boggling world?

In this book, we discussed the modes of thinking that Jesus applied. With this information in mind, how would you respond to the following challenges in our post-modern life:

1. Geoffrey Hinton did pioneering work in the area of Artificial Intelligence (AI). However, he now quitted his job so that he can speak freely about the dangers of technology. By applying **SYSTEM THINKING**, what would you imagine could be some of the most radical and unforeseen dangers that we may face when technology develops further?
2. Use colourful **METAPHORS** to describe the place of Twitter in our modern society.
3. Describe the role of social media in **PARADOXICAL** statements.
4. Do you think that in the nearby future robots would be able to act on **INTUITION** as well?
5. By using **IMAGE STREAMING**, think creatively about new areas where ChatGPT can be employed.
6. You are a teacher, and the students play with their cell phones while you are lecturing. How would you handle this as a **WHOLE BRAIN THINKER?**
7. You are an **OUT OF THE BOX THINKER**. What function would you develop for a multi-function watch which is not yet found on a watch, and which could make our lives much easier?

"Every tomorrow has two handles. We can take hold of it with the handle of anxiety or the handle of faith."

– Henry Ward Beecher

www.ingramcontent.com/pod-product-compliance
Lightning Source LLC
Chambersburg PA
CBHW070307010526
44107CB00056B/2517